cypress

Craig Deihl
Photographs by Rick McKee

Wyrick & Company

AN IMPRINT OF GIBBS SMITH, PUBLISHER

Salt Lake City | Charleston | Santa Fe | Santa Barbara

First Edition
10 09 08 07   5 4 3 2 1

Published by Wyrick & Company
An imprint of Gibbs Smith, Publisher
P.O. Box 667
Layton, UT 84041

1.800.748.5439 orders
www.gibbs-smith.com

Designed by Deibra McQuiston
Printed and bound in China

Library of Congress Cataloging-in-Publication Data

Deihl, Craig.
  Cypress / Craig Deihl ;
photographs by Rick McKee. — 1st ed.
      p. cm.
  Includes bibliographical references and index.
  ISBN-13: 978-0-941711-88-3 (alk. paper)
  ISBN-10: 0-941711-88-9 (alk. paper)
  1. Cookery, Asian. 2. Cookery, American—Southern style. 3.
Cypress
Lowcountry Grille. I. Title.

TX724.5.A1D44 2007
641.5'95—dc22

2006030799

For Mom and Dad

You taught me the values of hard work and determination. You
provided me with an education. You made me what I am today.

For my wife Colleen

None of this would be possible without you. You understand
my life as a chef. You are my biggest fan. I love you.

acknowledgments

I owe thanks to so many people for shaping this book into what it has become. I hope all of you are as proud as I am of the final results.

I would like to thank Tom Parsell and Donald Barickman for giving me the opportunity of running their restaurant at the age of 23. You took a huge risk. That risk was by far the most challenging for me to face, for I didn't want to fail. Thank you for all the support that went into Cypress and this book.

The sous chefs and management team that held up standards while I was working on this book. Without you it would not have been possible.

All staff members of Cypress, both past and present. You shaped this restaurant and for that I am forever indebted to you. I provided the ideas and you made them a reality. You all make me look good.

M. Kelly Wilson, the pastry chef of Cypress. Your continuous work at making your fabulous desserts. You had a huge role in completing them and they are awesome.

Anne Pope, you spent hours listening to me go on about food, flavors, and techniques then turned them into written text. You make this book read as I only dreamed it would. I know how hard you worked pushing me along, and for that I am grateful.

Rick McKee, the man behind the lens. You captured the food as I could only imagine. You shot the anatomy of what makes up great food. You showed the cooking process in a way I could not describe.

Pete Wyrick and Christopher Robbins, for seeing the potential at making the project a reality. You also took a huge risk at publishing an unknown. You have no idea how much that means to me.

The entire staff of Gibbs Smith did an outstanding job putting together this fascinating book. You made my hard work and dedication a reality.

Finally, I'd like to thank my family. Colleen, I know how hard it is for you putting up with me as a chef. Then, I added the book and things went into overdrive. You hardly saw me for a month, but you kept giving me the encouragement I needed to get it done. That's why I love you!

Mom and Dad, you understand the restaurant environment, yet neither of you have ever had a kitchen job. You have no idea how the two of you have shaped my life.

contents

10 FOREWORD

12 PREFACE

16 INTRODUCTION

20 THE CYPRESS PANTRY

28 STOCKS

36 1 RAW

50 2 APPETIZERS

82 3 SALADS AND CHEESE

104 4 SOUPS AND STEWS

122 5 FISH AND SHELLFISH

150 6 POULTRY AND FOWL

166 7 MEATS

200 8 ACCOMPANIMENTS

212 9 DESSERTS

238 COOKING TECHNIQUES

243 TESTING AND MEASUREMENTS

244 WINE PAIRINGS

250 SOURCES

251 INDEX

foreword

When I was asked to write the foreword for Craig's first cookbook, I felt as if I would be writing about someone who is in the early stages of what will become a famously well known career in food. Craig is undoubtedly one of the nation's most talented young chefs, and we are fortunate to have him at the helm of Cypress Lowcountry Grille.

After four years of working diligently at Magnolias while earning his culinary degree from Johnson & Wales University, Craig made it clear that he had his sights set on his next move. It just so happened that we were putting together our newest and most adventurous restaurant concept: Cypress. Knowing that this fiery 23-year-old chef's true talent would rise to the top, we put Craig in charge soon after the restaurant opened. He thrived on the challenge, injecting his own culinary style and management principles, helping to create what has become one of Charleston's premier fine dining restaurants.

The hospitality business is well known for having people come and go. Craig is unique: he has always been on the ascent. Separating himself from the average line cook, who works hard and plays even harder, Craig always pushed frivolous after-hours activities aside, making time to research the most current food trends, cooking methods and techniques. His singular focus on food has served him well. Craig's cuisine is abreast of some of the country's most successful chefs. Many are his personal favorites and mentors, and with several of whom he has staged, such as Alfred Portale, Thomas Keller, Charlie Trotter, Patrick O'Connell, Nobu Matsuhitsa, Tom Colicchio, Grant Achatz, Eric Ripert, Wylie Dufresne and Masaharu Morimoto.

Here are a few words to describe Craig and his philosophy: dedicated, curious, passionate, driven, knowledgeable, experimental, daring,

and precise. His dazzling recipes of indigenous ingredients, flavor combinations and textures all reflect his sacrosanct flavor rule of "hot, sour, salty, sweet, and sometimes bitter." Fresh local ingredients are of the utmost importance to Craig, and he is in constant contact with our local farmers giving input as to what needs to be planted based on the upcoming season and his menu. From elegant dishes such as Short Ribs and Lobster, Foie Gras with French Toast, Lobster and Truffle Grits to more modern concepts like Wasabi Tuna and Serrano-Wrapped Mahi-mahi, Craig is adept at marrying local cuisine with the exotic. With a love of fire, he has mastered Cypress's wood-burning grill to resurrect forgotten tableside classics including Châteaubriand and the popular Rack of Lamb with a Garlic Herb Rub .

I am exceedingly proud of Craig's accomplishments in the kitchen and within our company. Working with him has taught me many great things and has given me a different approach to food over the years. This book is a testament to his dedication and enthusiasm for the culinary arts, and knowing Craig as I do, it's only a preview of what's to come!

Donald Barickman
Founding Executive Chef/Managing Partner
Hospitality Management Group, Inc.

preface

In this book, Chef Craig Deihl will take you on a fascinating journey through his culinary world. As a prelude to that, I would like to recount the chronology of significant events that provided a platform for Craig's rapid climb to Executive Chef of Cypress Lowcountry Grille.

In 1990, I formed Hospitality Management Group, Inc., with Chef Donald Barickman, to build and open Magnolias Uptown/Down South. Today, that restaurant is a culinary landmark. Chef Barickman is credited as being Charleston's pioneer of lowcountry cuisine and has two published cookbooks on the subject. It is in this environment that Chef Deihl first came to our company as a 17-year-old culinary student.

In 1993, Barickman and I built Blossom, a more casual dining concept. Today, Blossom is a thriving seafood restaurant located between Magnolias and Cypress.

In 1999, I purchased the property next to Blossom. This magnificent building offered an unprecedented restaurant opportunity in Charleston's historic district. On the prominent corner of East Bay and Queen streets, the two-storied structure was an architectural gem dating back to 1834. It was our challenge and mission to retain the historic details and incorporate them with elegant modern elements in the interior. It was quite an adventure to find mortar scars in the ceiling from the siege of Charleston in 1864–65 and to uncover soaring walls built of bricks from the ballast of old English ships.

With the guidance of Atlanta Architect Bill Johnson (himself a native Charlestonian), Cypress evolved into the fitting backdrop for Chef Deihl's exciting new cuisine. From the three-story wine wall displaying over 5,000 bottles to the expo kitchen that can be viewed from two different stories, we were poised to take the Charleston dining experience to another level.

Chef Deihl had long demonstrated his outstanding culinary talent during his years at Magnolias. So, at the age of 23, Craig joined forces with Donald Barickman to create the menu for Cypress. Like the synergy of old and new within the building itself, Cypress's menu features many classic dishes updated for today's generation of discerning diners. From the restaurant's opening in April 2001 to today, Chef Deihl continues to display his mastery of the culinary arts. In the following pages, you will discover a new level of creative cooking achieved through methods that you can easily utilize in your own kitchen.

Thomas J. Parsell, President
Hospitality Management Group, Inc.
Magnolias/Blossom/Cypress

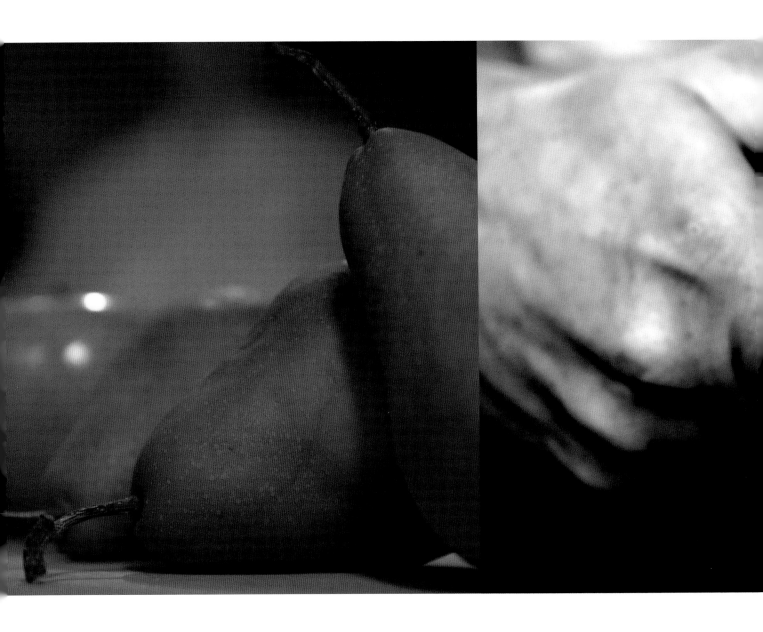

introduction

Like the hundreds of recipes that my staff and I prepare each evening for our guests at Cypress Lowcountry Grille, my own journey from an early interest in cooking to Cypress Executive Chef is ever-evolving. In *Cypress*, you will discover my culinary philosophy: that each new encounter with an ingredient is unique, and that there is no "right" way to cook. Cooking for me is a sensory experience and plated dishes are the end result of creative thought, problem solving and trained taste buds.

At Cypress, we begin with the finest amenities. Our facility and equipment are first class and, most importantly, we use fresh ingredients and hire creative capable chefs to execute our acclaimed menu of "global fusion" cuisine. With lowcountry ingredients in the lead, we use international cooking techniques—from classic French sautés to Asian tempura—and layer our distinctive flavors, so that each menu item reveals a symphony of hot, sour, salty, sweet, and bitter.

Test the recipes and recommendations that follow. Meld them into your own kitchen environment and adapt them to your region's produce, meats, seafood and specialties. Become your own kitchen's executive chef and delight in the rewards of sharing food with family and friends!

From the time I could hold a pot, my mother Joann taught me kitchen basics and began to pass on her extensive knowledge of food and cooking. Community cookbooks and recipes from friends and

family are her culinary guides for solid dishes such as boiled ham, green beans and potatoes. My father Dan introduced my brother Aaron and me to the art of slow roast grilling as a means of cooking the fruits of our surrounding woods and waters including fresh venison and trout. Our family lives in Danville, Pennsylvania, a country town where the dinner hour is sacred and families share the nightly meal and conversation about the day. Gathering and preparing food was a central factor in my upbringing. My grandfather (known as the "Melon King") owns a 90-acre farm and I worked summers in the fields where he raised melons and sweet corn, among other crops. Cooking breakfast and baking became my key interests and at age fourteen I was thrilled to receive a Kitchen Aid standup mixer for Christmas—highly unusual for a teenage boy, but I still use it today!

My first kitchen job was at the Pine Barn Inn, Danville's leading "white tablecloth" restaurant. I was 15 and not legally allowed in the kitchen; at the start, I bused tables and carved the steamship round as it was served in the dining room. At 16, I was allowed into the inner sanctum of the kitchen, and it was there that I learned the cadence, cost efficiencies and the nuts and bolts of running a restaurant.

From this point, my personal experience and professional life became inextricably intertwined; I knew that I was destined for a career in culinary arts. Over the course of high school, I jumped at the chance to take cooperative classes at Columbia Montour Area Vocational School where I participated in statewide and national cooking competitions, earning a college scholarship to Johnson & Wales University. I arrived at the school's Charleston, South Carolina, campus ten days after high school graduation and quickly learned that I much preferred practical, hands-on classes to lectures. I was motivated to take on a part-time job, and fellow students recommended Magnolias as one of the best restaurants in town. Here, under the tutelage of talented chefs. including Hospitality Management Group's (HMGI) Founding Chef/Managing Partner Donald Barickman, Executive Chef Don Drake, and chefs Mike Dragon, Brian Lindsay, and John Wright, I expanded my knowledge of the restaurant business, learning the role of kitchen stations, costing dishes, scheduling and management.

I moved to Cypress (HMGI's third Charleston restaurant) in 2001 to help design the kitchen and oversee the opening process; I was named Executive Chef six months after the opening. Donald and owner Thomas Parsell saw the fire within and gave me an opportunity to shine with my own style of cuisine backed by a world-class wine program and their business expertise. We have since earned accolades from the nation's leading food critics and, most importantly, the dining community in Charleston and beyond.

With this cookbook, I hope to teach and inspire readers with what I have learned over the past fifteen years of working as a home cook, in kitchens large and small, and today as executive chef of Cypress Lowcountry Grille, which I am proud to say is undoubtedly one of Charleston's most acclaimed fine dining establishments. Enjoy!

HOW TO USE THIS BOOK

As the Executive Chef of Cypress, I have written this cookbook with the intention of sharing some of the restaurant's favorite dishes, as well as to give the home cook a comprehensive guide on cooking "Cypress style" with my favorite ingredients and techniques. The recipes are exact; read the entire recipe before you begin!

Mis en place is a French term meaning "everything in its place." These are words that the staff of Cypress lives by. Every item is always in the same spot. Prep work is always done the same way and put in the same location. This allows us to be quick and efficient in the always fast-paced kitchen.

After you read through an entire recipe, start on the ingredients prep. Put all of your prep (chopped vegetables, spices, herbs, etc.) into small bowls or containers and set them out according to the sequence in which they will be used. Some of your prep can be done a day or more in advance; some will need to be done *à la minute*, meaning "at the last minute." Have your prep and *mis en place* completed before you begin cooking. It will make your work easier and it's also a great way to impress guests when you entertain!

As you master these recipes, look at the book and its contents in a general way. Take in the recipes and recommendations as a guide to set you on the path to becoming a stellar home cook.

I urge you to learn the basic culinary principles, including organizational planning, cooking techniques, and my flavor profiles: hot, sour, salty, sweet, and bitter. From there, put your own five senses in gear and create a personal repertoire of recipes and flavor combinations that will become the requested meals from your own kitchen.

the cypress pantry

At Cypress it goes without saying that we always use the freshest "in-season" ingredients when preparing food, and I encourage you to do the same in your kitchen at home. The quality of the ingredients is key to the success of the dish! This rule of thumb does require a little extra work on the front end—sourcing your area's best fishmonger and butcher, scouring the weekly farmers markets for the best produce—but your efforts will pay off in incredibly flavorful food that will continually please your family and even the most discerning "foodie" friends.

ASIAN CONDIMENTS——Add an eye-opening color and decadence of ginger, cilantro, citrus soy and chili glaze, transforming simplicity into new sweet and savory meals.

BLACK BEAN SOY

2 cups water
¼ cup fermented black beans (find in Asian section
   of market)
1 cup soy sauce
¼ cup mirin
3 tablespoons honey
1 tablespoon lime juice
1 tablespoon chopped cilantro
1 tablespoon chopped ginger
1 clove garlic, chopped

1.   Combine water and fermented black beans and soak overnight.
2.   Strain black beans through a fine sieve and press lightly. Discard liquid, as it will be very salty.
3.   Combine the beans and remaining ingredients in a saucepan and place over medium heat and cook for 8 minutes.
4.   Remove from heat, and strain through a fine sieve. Press lightly on the vegetables to release a little pulp from the beans. Keep liquid, discarding vegetables and beans.
5.   Sauce can be kept for 1 week.

CHILI GLAZE

½ cup honey
2 tablespoons sambal
3 tablespoons rice wine vinegar
1 tablespoon fine sea salt

Combine all ingredients in a non-reactive bowl and incorporate evenly. This sauce can be kept at room temperature for about a week.

CITRUS SOY

1 cup soy sauce
½ cup rice wine vinegar
1 tablespoon sambal
2 cloves garlic
½ cup sugar
3 tablespoons honey
2 tablespoons diced fresh ginger
1 tablespoon chopped cilantro
1 lemon, zest and juice
1 lime, zest and juice
1 orange, zest and juice

1.   Place all ingredients in a heavy-bottom saucepan and reduce over medium heat by half.
2.   When reduced, strain and cool. The soy can be made a day or two ahead of time; be sure to keep it cold.

YIELDS 2 CUPS

CHILI SOY SAUCE

½ cup Citrus Soy (see above)
½ cup Chili Glaze (see above)

1.   Combine ingredients evenly.
2.   Keep refrigerated.

CHINESE FIVE SPICE POWDER

1 tablespoon Szechwan peppercorn
1 tablespoon star anise
1 tablespoon cloves
1 tablespoon cinnamon stick
1 tablespoon fennel seed

1. Add the spices to a spice grinder and pulse until fine powder. You may want to sift this if you can't grind it fine enough.
2. Place in a tightly sealed container and use as soon as possible.

CHILI GARLIC GLAZE

¼ cup rice wine vinegar
½ cup sugar
1 tablespoon fine sea salt
1 tablespoon minced garlic
1 tablespoon minced ginger
½ tablespoon sambal oelek
½ tablespoon chopped cilantro
½ tablespoon chopped mint
½ tablespoon chopped basil

YIELDS ½ CUP

1. In a saucepan, combine rice wine vinegar, sugar and salt. Place over medium-high heat and reduce by one-fourth. Mixture should have a syrup-like consistency.
2. Remove from heat and add garlic, ginger and sambal. Incorporate evenly and allow mixture to cool completely.
3. Add cilantro, mint and basil to cooled mixture. (Adding herbs to a hot mixture will cause the herbs to turn brown.)
4. Place in a container and keep refrigerated.

HERBS——The herbs listed throughout this book are all fresh. If you do not work with fresh herbs now, I urge you to become familiar with them. You can grow them at home in small pots or you can find them in the produce section of your market. Wash them the same way you would lettuce or other greens.

Stripping Herbs: Hold the stem between your thumbs and index fingers and pull the stem, slowly stripping the leaves off. Discard the stem. The leaves can then be chopped or added directly to the item that you are preparing.

SALTS——Different salts perform on different levels. Here is a list of my preferred salts and how they are best used:

Kosher Salt: Readily available and my favorite all-purpose salt.

Fine Sea Salt: Best for frying, as the fine grain sticks to the product.

Maldon Sea Salt: This salt from the coast of England is too pricey for frying, but great for seasoning raw fish recipes and beef tartare.

Fleur de Sel and Sel Gris: Coarse sea salts such as these are used to finish meat and fish.

Rock Salt: Used for the presentation of some of our raw dishes.

OILS—In many of my recipes, I call for olive oil, extra virgin olive oil, walnut oil, peanut oil and canola oil. Each of these is mentioned by name, as they are specific to the preparation. At Cypress, our olive oil is actually a blend of canola oil and extra virgin olive oil, as it yields a better flavor when sautéing.

There are many different types of extra virgin olive oil, so many that you will need to taste them individually and find your own favorite. Only a little is needed, and I suggest that you buy small bottles so that the oil stays fresh.

INFUSED OILS AND COMPOUND BUTTERS.
Infused oils are made by blanching herbs and puréeing with oil to infuse with flavor and vibrant color. These oils not only add visual appeal, but also add a flavorful note to a variety of meat, fish and vegetable dishes.

BASIL OIL
2 cups basil leaves, stems removed
½ cup canola oil
¼ cup extra virgin olive oil

1. Blanch the basil leaves in boiling water for 20 seconds and then plunge into ice water. Using paper towels, dry the basil as much as possible.
2. Combine the basil and the canola oil in a blender and purée for 5 minutes. You will see steam coming out of the blender. This is normal.
3. Finish the basil oil by adding the extra virgin olive oil and purée for 10 seconds.
4. Place the oil in a small clear container, refrigerate and allow to settle overnight. This will intensify the flavor.
5. Before using, bring the oil back to room temperature. This will make it easier to decant. Also, the oil tends to solidify when chilled.
6. Decant the oil by removing the clear oil from the top. When all the oil is removed, place the remaining amount in a coffee filter and allow to settle.

MINT OIL
2 cups mint leaves, stems removed
½ cup grape seed oil

1. Blanch the mint leaves in boiling water for 20 seconds and then plunge into ice water. Using paper towels, dry the mint as much as possible.
2. Combine the mint and grape seed oil in a blender and purée for 5 minutes. You will see steam coming out of the blender. This is normal.
3. Place the oil in a small clear container, refrigerate and allow to settle overnight. This will intensify the mint flavor.
4. Before using, bring the oil back to room temperature. This will make it easier to decant. Also, the oil tends to solidify when chilled.
5. Decant the oil by removing the clear oil from the top. When all the oil is removed, place the remaining amount in a coffee filter and allow to settle.

CHIVE OIL
2 cups chives
½ cup canola oil
¼ cup extra virgin olive oil

1. Blanch the chives in boiling water for 20 seconds and then plunge into ice water. Using paper towels, dry the chives as much as possible.
2. Combine the chives and the canola oil in a blender and purée for 5 minutes. You will see steam coming out of the blender. This is normal.
3. Finish the chive oil by adding the extra virgin olive oil and purée for 10 seconds.
4. Place the oil in a small clear container, refrigerate and allow to settle overnight. This will intensify the flavor.
5. Before using, bring the oil back to room temperature. This will make it easier to decant. Also, the oil tends to solidify when chilled.
6. Decant the oil by removing the clear oil from the top. When all the oil is removed, place the remaining amount in a coffee filter and allow to settle.

HERB OIL

½ cup sage leaves, stems removed
½ cup rosemary, stems removed
½ cup thyme leaves, stems removed
½ cup flat-leaf parsley, stems removed
1 cup canola oil
¼ cup extra virgin olive oil

1. Combine the herbs and blanch for 20 seconds and then plunge into ice water. Using paper towels, dry the herbs as much as possible.
2. Place the herbs and the canola oil in a blender and purée for 5 minutes. You will see steam coming out of the blender. This is normal.
3. Finish the herb oil by adding the extra virgin olive oil and purée for 10 seconds.
4. Place the oil in a small clear container, refrigerate and allow to settle overnight. This will intensify the flavor of the herbs.
5. Before using, bring the oil back to room temperature. This will make it easier to decant. Also, the oil tends to solidify when chilled.
6. Decant the oil by removing the clear oil from the top. When all the oil is removed, place the remaining amount in a coffee filter and allow to settle.

BUTTERS——Everything's better with butter. That said, it is important to know that there is butter (containing 80 percent butter fat) and there is good butter. The recipes in this book should be made with the "good" butter—usually a European style, unsalted, with 82 percent butter fat. This 2 percent makes an enormous difference, as you are getting more whole butter and less of the flavorless milk solids that are emulsified into (80 percent) butter. The "good" butter is a little more expensive, but readily available at upscale grocery stores. My favorite brand is Plúgra, but there are others you might try.

SQUASH BLOSSOM BUTTER

½ pound unsalted butter, room temperature
16 zucchini or squash blossoms, chopped
½ tablespoon sea salt
1 teaspoon white pepper
1 tablespoon honey

This recipe is a prime example of making use of everything edible. One spring, I received an order of squash blossoms and they were badly mishandled. But, they were bought and paid for and I wasn't about to throw them away. The resourceful chef in me put the blossoms in the food processor with some butter and puréed them for an aromatic butter to use for finishing vegetables or fish dishes. The way I see it, everything is better with butter.

1. Combine all ingredients in a food processor. Purée until smooth. Scrape the sides of the bowl and purée again until you have a consistent mixture.
2. Divide butter between two 10-inch squares of food film and roll into logs.
3. Refrigerate butter and use within 1 week, or place in the freezer and use within 4 months.

LEMON BUTTER

½ pound unsalted butter, room temperature
3 tablespoons lemon zest
2 tablespoons lemon juice
½ tablespoon salt
1 teaspoon white pepper

1. Combine all ingredients in a food processor. Purée until smooth. Scrape the sides of the bowl and purée again until you have a consistent mixture.
2. Divide butter between two 10-inch squares of food film and roll into logs.
3. Refrigerate butter and use within 1 week, or place in the freezer and use within 4 months.

TRUFFLE BUTTER

½ **pound unsalted butter, room temperature**
4 **tablespoons truffle peelings packed in oil**
½ **tablespoon salt**
1 **teaspoon white pepper**
1 **tablespoon honey**

1.   Combine all ingredients in a food processor. Purée until smooth. Scrape the sides of the bowl and purée again until you have a consistent mixture.
2.   Divide butter between two 10-inch squares of food film and roll into logs.
3.   Refrigerate butter and use within one week, or place in the freezer and use in 4 months.

HERB BUTTER

1 **tablespoon butter**
1 **tablespoon chopped garlic**
1 **tablespoon chopped shallots**
½ **pound unsalted butter, room temperature**
2 **tablespoons finely chopped rosemary**
2 **tablespoons finely chopped thyme**
2 **tablespoons minced chives**

1.   Place a sauté pan over medium-low heat. When hot, add the butter, garlic and shallots and sweat. Stir the mixture often so that it does not caramelize.
2.   When the garlic and shallots become translucent, remove from heat and allow to cool.
3.   Combine unsalted butter and garlic mixture in a food processor. Purée until smooth. Scrape the sides of the bowl and purée again until you have a consistent mixture.
4.   Fold the herbs into the butter and incorporate evenly.
5.   Divide butter between two 10-inch squares of food film and roll into logs.
6.   Refrigerate butter and use within one week, or place in the freezer and use within 4 months.

CLARIFIED BUTTER

2 **pounds butter**

Clarified butter is not a mystery, but is butter with the milk solids removed, leaving you with pure butter fat. It has a high smoke point and works great for sautéing. It's mostly used to make Hollandaise and other sauces, sometimes for desserts. If you are going to the trouble of making this recipe, double it and freeze what you don't use for the next cooking session.

1.   Add the butter to a saucepan and place over medium heat.
2.   When the butter begins to simmer remove from heat. Skim all the foam from the top of the butter.
3.   Remove and save the clear liquid on top. This is the clarified butter. Discard the milky liquid at the bottom.

YIELDS 3 CUPS

DRY SPICES—Dry spices play an important role in our Cypress cuisine. I recommend that you buy your own spices in small quantities, as you will use them in small amounts and they go stale over time. Dry spices may be toasted for depth of flavor, and a spice grinder is a good tool to have on hand for making powders and small batches of spiced oils.

RICE, GRAINS AND PASTAS—We use very little pasta at Cypress. Udon, buckwheat and rice noodles—more Asian than Italian—are the extent of our pasta offerings. We do, however, use a range of grains from stone-ground grits to hominy corn. Our rice runs the gamut from Carolina Gold to Arborio for risottos and short grain sushi rice.

LEMON CONFIT
8 lemons
¼ cup lemon juice
¼ cup salt
¼ cup sugar

This condiment can be frozen and kept on hand at all times.

1.   Cut the lemons into quarters and mix with the remaining ingredients.
2.   Place into a quart-size jar or other container with a tight lid.
3.   Place the jar in the refrigerator. Shake the jar to incorporate the ingredients evenly; do this every day for one week.
4.   The lemons can be stored in the refrigerator for one week or frozen for up to 4 months. If freezing, place the lemons and syrup in a resealable bag and place within another resealable bag to prevent leakage.

YIELDS 1 QUART

SOFFRITO
½ cup fennel, trimmed to bulb and minced
½ cup minced garlic
½ cup minced onion
¾ cup extra virgin olive oil
Use fronds for garnish

The fennel and garlic can be minced with a food processor. The onion must be minced by hand; the food processor will make the onion too wet.

1.   Cut the fennel bulb in half and remove the core. Cut the fennel into small pieces and place in a food processor and mince fine.
2.   Repeat the same process with the garlic.
3.   In a saucepan, combine all the ingredients. Place over medium heat and bring to a simmer.
4.   When a simmer has been reached, lower the temperature and allow the mixture to sweat. Stir the mixture every couple of minutes to prevent sticking.
5.   As the liquid evaporates, the vegetables will caramelize. This will take 30 to 40 minutes.
6.   When the mixture starts to caramelize, cook for 5 minutes. The mixture should be light brown in color.
7.   Remove from heat and let cool in the pan. When cool, place in a container for later use. Soffrito can be frozen for up to 4 months.

stocks

Stocks are the backbone of the cuisine at Cypress, adding nuances of flavor to nearly everything on our menu. We almost always have a stock simmering on the range or in our monstrous forty-gallon kettle. Our batch sizes are typically ten times the amount yielded by the recipes that follow. (In other words, we're making 140-pound batches of veal stock that cook for more than 36 hours at a time and yield nearly ten gallons.) Great stocks are important to me as a cook because they are the building blocks of exceptional cuisine. They are also versatile ingredients that can add instant panache to a dish. For example, veal stock added to recipes for fish dishes such as wreckfish or salmon gives a richer, more robust flavor.

VEAL STOCK

12 pounds veal bones
Water
1½ cups onion, large chop
½ cup leeks, large chop
1 cup carrots, large chop

1 cup celery, large chop
1 garlic bulb, cut in half
6 sprigs parsley
12 sprigs thyme
6 sprigs rosemary

4 bay leaves
15 black peppercorns
1½ cups tomato paste
2 gallons water

I know! I know! You're thinking that veal bones are expensive, hard to find and that you don't have a pot large enough to cook them in. I still urge you to make this stock, as there really isn't a substitute. Well, you can take some shortcuts, but we will get to that later (roasted chicken stock fortified with veal stew meat). The first stock is very neutral in flavor and provides extra body for use in other stocks or for fortifying roasted scraps; this is why I don't add tomato paste to it.

The second running is called a "rémoulage" and contains tomato paste, which helps provide a deeper color and richer flavor. We then combine both stocks together and reduce by half. With the reduced stock, we can create numerous classic sauces.

1. Place the veal bones in a large stockpot (20 quart or larger). Add enough water to cover the veal bones and move them around to loosen any coagulated blood or bone fragments, [1]. Drain the water off of the veal bones.
2. Cover the veal bones with cold water. Add the remaining ingredients, making sure there is at least 2 inches left between the ingredients and the top of the pot to allow for expansion. Place the stockpot on the stove over medium-low heat. This is the temperature that the stock will remain for the entire time it cooks.

3. As the water begins to simmer, a scum will start to form at the top; remove the scum, [2]. Pull the stockpot slightly off the heat; this will allow a slow convective movement that moves the scum to one side of the pot for easy skimming. Cook the stock for at least 8 hours; run overnight if you can. Continue to skim.
4. Remove the stockpot from the heat and allow it to cool. Strain the stock through a chinois into another pot, reserving the veal bones in the stockpot, [3]. Place the strained stock back on the stove over medium heat and bring to a simmer. Once again, continue to skim the scum and fat off of the top. Reduce the stock by half.
5. Combine the tomato paste and water and incorporate evenly. Add this to the veal bones and return the pot to medium-low heat. Pull the stockpot slightly off the heat and cook for 4 hours.
6. Turn off the heat to the stockpot and allow it to cool. Strain the stock through a chinois into another pot. Discard the real bones. Reduce this stock by half.
7. When both stocks are reduced by half, combine them and reduce by half.
8. Remove from heat and shock in an ice bath. When cold, place in small containers and refrigerate for up to 1 week or freeze for up to 6 months, [4].

YIELDS 2 GALLONS

CHICKEN STOCK

8 pounds chicken bones, backs, wings (no skin or fat) Water 1 cup onion, large chop	1 cup leeks, large chop ½ cup celery, large chop ½ cup carrots, large chop 1 garlic bulb, dried skin removed, cut in half 5 sprigs parsley	10 sprigs thyme 4 sprigs sage 4 bay leaves 10 white peppercorns

This is one stock that I strongly urge you to make from scratch and always have on hand in your freezer. It isn't expensive like veal stock and the bones aren't hard to find. This is a good stock to fortify with veal stew meat to create a veal stock substitute. Or you can roast the bones following the duck stock recipe.

1. Using a cleaver, cut the chicken bones into small pieces. Wash the bones with cold water to remove blood and small bone fragments.
2. In a large stockpot (16 quart or larger), place the chicken bones. Completely cover the chicken bones with cold water by at least 2 inches. Place stockpot over medium-low heat and bring to a simmer. This will take about 1 hour; skim any scum that comes to the surface.
3. Add the onion, leeks, celery, carrots, and garlic to the stockpot. Top off the mirepoix with the parsley, thyme, sage, bay leaves, and peppercorns. As the water begins to simmer, a scum will start to form at the top; remove the scum. Pull the stockpot slightly off the heat; this will allow a slow convective movement that moves the scum to one side of the pot for easy removal. Continue skimming frequently. Cook the stock for at least 6 hours.
4. Turn off the heat to the stockpot and allow it to cool slowly. Strain the stock through a chinois into another large stockpot. Place the stockpot with the stock in it back on the stove over medium heat and bring to a simmer. Continue to skim the scum and fat off of the top. Reduce the stock by half.
5. Remove from heat and shock in an ice bath. When cold, place in small containers and refrigerate for up to 1 week or freeze for up to 4 months.

YIELDS 2 GALLONS

CORN STOCK

8 ears of sweet corn 1/2 cup chopped onion 1/2 cup chopped celery 1 cup sherry	5 white peppercorns 2 bay leaves 1/4 cup basil	

This stock utilizes corn bones. Actually, they are just corncobs, but we use them in the same fashion as we would with bone stocks. The cobs contain a tremendous amount of corn flavor. We use the corn stock to make corn purees and as a base liquid for cooking grits and polenta.

1. Cut the corn off the cob. Save the corn kernels for later use.
2. In a large pot, combine corncobs and remaining ingredients.
3. Place the pot over medium heat and bring to a low simmer. Cook the corn stock for 1 hour.
4. Strain the stock into another pot and discard the corncobs. Return stock to medium heat and reduce by half.
5. This stock is best when used immediately; however, it can be frozen and used within 6 months.

YIELDS 4 CUPS

ROASTED DUCK STOCK

5 pounds duck bones, backs, wings (no skin or fat)	½ cup celery, large chop	10 sprigs thyme
Water	½ cup carrots, large chop	4 bay leaves
¾ cup onion, large chop	1 garlic bulb, dried skin removed, cut in half	10 white peppercorns
¾ cup leeks, large chop	5 sprigs parsley	

This stock is going to use the carcasses from the ducks you buy to make other recipes in this book. You can also ask your butcher to get just the bones for you. The bones are roasted to produce a richer flavor; this accents the duck more appropriately.

1. Preheat oven to 350 degrees.
2. Using a cleaver, cut the duck bones into small pieces. Wash the bones with cold water to remove blood and small bone fragments.
3. Place the duck bones in a roasting pan. Place the pan in the oven and roast for 1 hour. Move the bones around and roast for another 20 minutes. Remove the bones from the oven and add the bones to a large stockpot (16 quart or larger). Pour off the duck fat and save. Deglaze the pan by adding 4 cups of water. Place back in the oven for 3 to 4 minutes, remove the pan and scraping the bottom with a metal spatula to loosen the fond. Add this to the stockpot.
4. Cover the bones with cold water. Add the onion, leeks, celery, carrots, and garlic to the stockpot. Top off the mirepoix with the parsley, thyme, bay leaves, and peppercorns.
5. Place the stockpot over medium-low heat and bring to a simmer. As the water begins to simmer, a scum will start to form at the top; remove the scum. Pull the stockpot slightly off the heat; this will allow a slow convective movement that moves the scum to one side of the pot for easy removal. Continue skimming frequently. Cook the stock for at least 6 hours.
6. Turn off the heat to the stockpot and allow it to cool slowly. Strain the stock through a chinois into another large stockpot. Place the stockpot with the stock back on the stove over medium heat and bring to a simmer. Continue to skim the scum and fat off of the top. Reduce the stock by half.
7. Remove from heat and shock in an ice bath. When cold, place in small containers and refrigerate for up to 1 week or freeze for up to 4 months.

YIELDS 1½ GALLONS

SMOKED PORK STOCK

4 pounds smoked pork neck bones	¾ cup leeks, large chop	5 sprigs parsley
2 pounds smoked ham hocks	½ cup celery, large chop	10 sprigs thyme
Water	½ cup carrots, large chop	4 bay leaves
¾ cup onion, large chop	1 garlic bulb, dried skin removed, cut in half	10 white peppercorns

This stock is best described as "liquid bacon." I like to cook greens and various types of beans in this stock. In the south, we have the luxury of buying smoked pork bones in the grocery store. If you can't find them, ask your butcher to smoke some for you. Or smoke some yourself.

1.   In a large stockpot (16 quart or larger), place the pork bones and ham hocks. Completely cover the bones with cold water.
2.   Add the onion, leeks, celery, carrots, and garlic to the stockpot. Top off the mirepoix with the parsley, thyme, bay leaves, and peppercorns. Place stockpot over medium-low heat and bring to a simmer. As the water begins to simmer a scum will start to form at the top; remove the scum. Pull the stockpot slightly off the heat; this will allow a slow convective movement that moves the scum to one side of the pot for easy removal. Continue skimming frequently. Cook the stock for at least 6 hours.
3.   Turn off the heat to the stockpot and allow it to cool slowly. Strain the stock through a chinois into another large stockpot. Place the stockpot with the stock back on the stove over medium heat and bring to a simmer. Continue to skim the scum and fat off of the top. Reduce the stock by half.
4.   Remove from heat and shock in an ice bath. When cold, place in small containers and refrigerate for up to 1 week or freeze for up to 4 months.

YIELDS 1 GALLON

FORTIFIED STOCK (OR QUICK STOCK)

4 pounds smoked pork neck bones	¾ cup leeks, large chop	5 sprigs parsley
2 pounds smoked ham hocks	½ cup celery, large chop	10 sprigs thyme
Water	½ cup carrots, large chop	4 bay leaves
¾ cup onion, large chop	1 garlic bulb, dried skin removed, cut in half	10 white peppercorns

Fortified stock is produced when we use a base stock—whether it be veal or chicken—and finish it with roasted byproducts. These byproducts, or bone and meat scraps, come from quail wing tips, lamb saddle backbones and trimmings from any type of meat that is being butchered. This is also a good way to create a stock from your Thanksgiving turkey carcass.

1.   Preheat oven to 350 degrees.
2.   Mix scraps and oil in a roasting pan. Roast 20 minutes.
3.   Strain off fat. Add onion, leeks and garlic and roast for another 5 minutes.
4.   Deglaze with wine, scraping the bottom of the pan to remove the fond.
5.   Place vegetables and scraps in a saucepan and add stock. Cook over medium-low heat for 20 minutes.
6.   Strain stock though a chinois and return to a low simmer. Using a ladle, skim any scum or fat that comes to the top.
7.   Season to taste with salt and pepper.
8.   Stock is now ready for use or can be stored in refrigerator or freezer.

YIELDS 1 GALLON

SHELLFISH STOCK

¼ cup extra virgin olive oil	2 (1¼–pound) lobsters, shells and juices only (see	1 cup white wine
½ cup onion, medium dice	lobster cooking process on p. 79)	½ cup tarragon
¼ cup celery, medium dice	½ pound shrimp shells	½ cup basil
¼ cup carrots, medium dice	½ cup tomato paste	1 tablespoon white peppercorns
1 head garlic, cut in half	½ cup brandy	8 cups water

Please don't ever throw lobster and shrimp shells away. Use them to make this stock and freeze it for when you need it. You can fortify the next set of shells with the one you have in the freezer.

1. Place a stockpot (8 quart or larger) over medium-high heat; add olive oil, onion, celery, carrots, and garlic. Sauté until caramelized (approximately 8 to 10 minutes).

2. Add the lobster and shrimp shells and juice from the broken down lobsters and caramelize (3 to 4 minutes). Add tomato paste and cook for another 5 to 6 minutes.

3. Deglaze with brandy and white wine. Stir, scrapping the bottom of the pan. Add tarragon, basil, peppercorns and water and cook for 30 minutes. Strain stock and discard lobster shells. Place stock back on stove and reduce by one-fourth.

YIELDS ½ GALLON

FISH FUMET

5 pounds fish bones, gills removed	½ cup celery, large chop	5 sprigs parsley
Water	½ cup carrots, large chop	10 sprigs thyme
¾ cup onion, large chop	¼ cup fennel, large chop	4 bay leaves
¾ cup leeks, large chop	1 garlic bulb, dried skin removed, cut in half	10 white peppercorns

Ask your fishmonger for the fish bones. I'm sure he will sell them real cheap. This mildly flavored broth is great for braising fish and shrimp, and using as a soup base, as in the oyster stew.

1. Wash the fish bones under cold water to remove excess blood and protein. You can soak them in saltwater overnight to remove even more blood.

2. Add the onion, leeks, celery, carrots, fennel and garlic to the stockpot. Top off with the parsley, thyme, bay leaves, and peppercorns. Place stockpot over medium-low heat and bring to a simmer. As the water begins to simmer, a scum will start to form at the top; remove the scum. Never bring this stock to a boil, as it will lose all clarity. Pull the stockpot slightly off the heat; this will allow a slow convective movement that moves the scum to one side of the pot for easy removal. Continue skimming frequently. Cook the stock for at least 2 hours.

3. Turn off the heat to the stockpot and allow it to cool slowly. Strain the stock through a chinois into another large stockpot. Place the stockpot with the stock back on the stove over medium heat and bring to a simmer. Continue to skim the scum and fat off of the top. Reduce the stock by one-third.

4. Remove from heat and shock in an ice bath. When cold, place in small containers and refrigerate for up to 1 week or freeze for up to 4 months.

YIELDS 1½ GALLONS

{ R A W } 1

the recipes

Sashimi Tuna and Kumomoto Oysters with Cilantro Lime Glaze and Pineapple Wasabi

Asian Tuna Tartare with Cucumbers, Chili Glaze, Shiitake Mushrooms and Chinese Flatbread

Bay Scallop Ceviche with Grape Tomatoes, Coriander and Lime

Fresh Oysters with Cucumber Lime Mignonette and Green Tomato-Wasabi Cocktail Sauce

Deconstructed Spicy Tuna Roll

Beef Tartare with Brioche Toast Points and Olive Oil

Hamiachi with Cucumber Noodles, Arugula, Yuzu Soy and Pink Peppercorn

T

The menu at Cypress begins with a fabulous selection of raw items as small bites and starters which are equally easy to prepare at home. Our raw foods—primarily proteins such as seafood and beef—are showcased within an iced raw bar at the front of the bustling kitchen. The display is impressive and emphasizes the importance of "raw" as revealing the true qualities of the foods' flavors. The house-made sauces and other accompaniments—from the Green Tomato-Wasabi Cocktail Sauce to Cilantro Lime Glaze—reflect our global cuisine and are tailored to complement each raw dish.

A word to the wise: it is of the utmost importance to treat raw proteins with care. Know your source. For seafood recipes, I recommend developing relationships with and placing orders through a local fishmonger so that the product is as fresh as possible. You may even do some research as to the best local suppliers whether they be at the docks or farmers market. Get to know your butcher; he can help educate you on fresher products and those that are to your specifications. If you've not tried a raw recipe in the past, dive in! This form of cuisine provides distinctive flavors in their truest form—an experience not to be missed.

SASHIMI TUNA AND KUMOMOTO OYSTERS
WITH CILANTRO LIME GLAZE AND PINEAPPLE WASABI

20 fresh Kumomoto oysters, in shell, stored on ice
Small bowl saltwater
1 pound sashimi grade tuna
4 cups crushed ice
Cilantro leaves

CILANTRO LIME GLAZE
½ tablespoon chopped cilantro
½ tablespoon chopped mint
2 tablespoons squeezed lime juice
½ teaspoon lime zest
3 tablespoons mirin
3 tablespoons rice wine vinegar
2 tablespoons fish sauce

2 tablespoons honey
1 teaspoon sambal (Sriracha Chili paste can be substituted)

PINEAPPLE WASABI
3 tablespoons pineapple juice
2 tablespoons ground wasabi powder

This recipe pops with the tantalizing tastes of hot, sour, salty and sweet. The creaminess of the oysters and tuna is offset by the zing of pineapple wasabi. On its own, the wasabi is pure heat, but the naturally sweet pineapple juice purée tones it down for a subtle, but important, kick.

1. Scrub the oysters free of dirt and debris, using a small brush.
2. Using an oyster knife, remove top shell of oyster; detach the bottom of the oyster, leaving it in the half shell. Check the oyster for any shell or grit. If there is excess grit, rinse with saltwater; otherwise leave the oyster in the shell.
3. Cut the tuna in 20 equal size blocks, about the same size as the oysters. Place the tuna on top of the oysters.

4. Place 1 teaspoon of the Cilantro Lime Glaze on top of the tuna. Finish with a small dot of the Pineapple Wasabi.
5. On four serving plates, place the crushed ice and top it with the cilantro leaves (this will keep the oysters cold and prevent them from sliding). Place 5 oysters on each plate on top of the cilantro and serve immediately.

FOR THE CILANTRO LIME GLAZE:
1. Combine all the ingredients in a small mixing bowl and incorporate evenly. Place in the refrigerator to chill.
2. The glaze can be made a day in advance.

FOR THE PINEAPPLE WASABI:
Combine pineapple juice and wasabi and incorporate evenly.

YIELDS 4 SERVINGS

ASIAN TUNA TARTARE

WITH CUCUMBERS, CHILI GLAZE, SHIITAKE MUSHROOMS AND CHINESE FLATBREAD

8 ounces tuna, small dice
½ cup cucumber, small dice
¼ cup sliced scallion
¼ cup Citrus Soy (see p. 22)
¼ cup Chili Glaze (see p. 22)

CHINESE FLATBREAD
8 egg roll wrappers
4 tablespoons canola oil
2 tablespoons Chinese Five Spice Powder
   (see p. 23)

SOY-GLAZED SHIITAKE MUSHROOMS
1 cup baby shiitake mushrooms
¼ cup Citrus Soy (see p. 22)

This popular appetizer—my first Asian-inspired recipe—was originally developed while I was working at Magnolias. It's light, but with intense fusion flavors and a striking presentation, making it a great start to a memorable meal.

1. In a mixing bowl combine tuna, cucumbers, scallions, and Citrus Soy; incorporate evenly, **[1] [2]**.
2. On four serving plates, place a 3-inch ring mold and one-fourth of the tuna mix, **[3]**. Press mix tightly. On each plate, insert 3 pieces of Chinese Flatbread, making a triangle, **[4]**. Carefully remove ring mold. Place 1 tablespoon Chili Glaze around the tartare. Finish with an equal amount of shiitake mushrooms and serve.

FOR THE CHINESE FLATBREAD:

1. Preheat oven to 325 degrees.
2. Cut egg roll wrappers in half. Lay both stacks on top of each other and cut in half again (to end up with rectangles).
3. Brush half the oil on a sheet tray. Place egg roll wrappers on greased tray. Brush wrappers with remaining oil. Sprinkle with Chinese Five Spice Powder.
4. Bake for 6 to 8 minutes, or until golden brown. Reserve for later. Flatbread should be made and used the same day.

FOR THE SOY-GLAZED SHIITAKE MUSHROOMS:

1. In a small saucepan combine the mushrooms and Citrus Soy. Place over medium heat and bring to a simmer.
2. Cook for 5 minutes. Cool mushrooms in the liquid. Refrigerate until ready to use.

YIELDS 4 SERVINGS

BAY SCALLOP CEVICHE
WITH GRAPE TOMATOES, CORIANDER AND LIME

1 pound dry-packed bay scallops
2 tablespoons coriander seed
1½ tablespoons salt
1 teaspoon white pepper

1½ cups lime juice (fresh squeezed)
2 tablespoons honey
4 scallions, green tops only
1 cup grape tomatoes

2 tablespoons chopped cilantro
¼ cup julienned red onion
2 tablespoons extra virgin olive oil

Bay scallops are a smaller variety—more texturally pleasing than the larger sea scallops. They pickle easily in the lime juice used for this summertime ceviche. A bit of honey neutralizes the acidity of the lime juice and tomatoes for a smoother, less tangy taste. This easy ceviche can be plated or served with chips as an hors d'oeuvre for al fresco cocktails.

1. In a mixing bowl, combine scallops, coriander seed, salt, and pepper. Mix until scallops are coated evenly. Let sit for 5 minutes.
2. Add the lime juice and honey and mix with the scallops.
3. Place in the refrigerator for at least 4 hours. This will allow the acid from the lime juice to pickle the scallops.
4. Cut the scallion tops into 2-inch lengths. Julienne tops thinly and place in cold water. The scallions will curl as they get cold.
5. Combine the tomatoes, cilantro, and red onion and incorporate with the scallops and lime juice.
6. In four serving bowls, place equal amounts of scallops and tomatoes. Place equal amounts of lime juice over the scallops. Finish with a drizzle of extra virgin olive oil.
7. Garnish with scallion curls and a drizzle of extra virgin olive oil.

YIELDS 4 SERVINGS

CHEF DEIHL'S NOTE: Seasoning the scallops before adding to the lime juice will allow the seasoning to stick to the scallops and become seasoned appropriately, versus adding it to the lime juice where all of the seasonings will fall to the bottom of the bowl.

FRESH OYSTERS WITH CUCUMBER LIME MIGNONETTE
AND GREEN TOMATO-WASABI COCKTAIL SAUCE

24 fresh oysters (in shell, stored on ice)
Small bowl saltwater
4 cups crushed ice
Sliced lemon quarters

CUCUMBER LIME MIGNONETTE
¼ cup cucumber, fine dice
¼ cup shallots, fine dice

½ teaspoon lime zest
1 tablespoon lime juice
¼ cup rice wine vinegar
1 teaspoon cracked white pepper
1 teaspoon fine sea salt

GREEN TOMATO-WASABI COCKTAIL SAUCE
1 cup green tomatoes, blanched, peeled and
    small dice

3 tablespoons sugar
3 tablespoons rice wine vinegar
2 teaspoons salt
2 tablespoons wasabi powder
3 tablespoons water
1 tablespoon grated fresh ginger
1 tablespoon chopped cilantro

We serve our oysters cold on the half shell. It's a traditional manner, but we've found it difficult to improve on the simple perfection of a salty East Coast select or the cucumber-creaminess of a West Coast variety. In addition to the classic lemon garnish, we offer the intensely flavored accompaniments featured here.

1. Scrub the oysters free of dirt and debris using a small brush, **[1]**.
2. Using an oyster knife, remove top shell of oyster; detach the bottom of the oyster, leaving it in the half shell. Check the oyster for any shell or grit, **[2]**. If there is excess grit, rinse with salt-water; otherwise leave the oyster in the shell, **[3]**.
3. On four serving platters, place the crushed ice. Place 6 oysters per plate on top of the crushed ice. Place a ramekin of each sauce and a slice of lemon on each plate and serve immediately.

FOR THE CUCUMBER LIME MIGNONETTE:
1. In a small mixing bowl combine all ingredients and incorporate well.
2. Refrigerate and serve chilled.

FOR THE GREEN TOMATO-WASABI COCKTAIL SAUCE:
1. In a small non-reactive saucepan, combine the tomatoes, sugar, vinegar and salt.
2. Place saucepan over medium-high heat and simmer for 3 to 4 minutes, or until the tomatoes start to break down.
3. Combine the wasabi and water to form a paste, making sure there are no lumps in the mixture.
4. Add the wasabi paste and the ginger to the tomatoes and cook over medium heat for 2 minutes.
5. Remove from heat and allow mixture to cool completely. When cool, add the cilantro and refrigerate.

YIELDS 4 SERVINGS

DECONSTRUCTED SPICY TUNA ROLL

RICE FOAM
½ cup Carolina Gold Rice
2 cups water
¼ cup rice wine vinegar
2 tablespoons mirin
3 tablespoons sugar

1 tablespoon salt
4 sheets gelatin (bloom in cold water)

TUNA
2 teaspoons sirachi (can substitute sambal)
¼ cup fresh pineapple
1 tablespoon fish sauce
½ pound diced sashimi tuna
4 sheets of nori

Cypress's artistic play on the popular spicy tuna roll is totally unique and a true "wow" item for guests. But be forewarned: this dish is more complicated than many of the other starters featured in this book. If you are up to the challenge of this recipe, plan ahead. Specifically, make sure you have the proper tools, including the ISI Gourmet Whip (a nitrous siphon) for the rice foam. The ISI is made for use with cold products and is available at Williams-Sonoma stores and Web site.

FOR THE RICE FOAM:

1. Combine Carolina Gold Rice and water in a small saucepan. Place on medium heat and cook. When water begins to boil, reduce heat to low and cook for 15 minutes. Rice mixture will be very wet.

2. Combine vinegar, mirin, sugar and salt in a small saucepan. Place over low heat to allow sugar and salt to dissolve. When dissolved, remove from heat.

3. Add rice mixture to blender and purée until smooth. Add vinegar and bloomed gelatin and blend with rice.

4. Strain mixture and place into a 1-quart foam canister.

5. Charge canister with 2 cartridges of nitrous. Allow mixture to chill overnight.

FOR THE TUNA:

1. Combine sirachi, pineapple and fish sauce in a food processor and purée until smooth. Strain this mixture. Refrigerate until very cold.

2. In a mixing bowl, combine tuna and cold spice mixture; incorporate evenly.

3. Crumble nori and place in a spice grinder. Grind to a powder. Use as soon as possible.

4. Place 2 tablespoons Rice Foam on four serving plates. In the center of the rice foam, place one-fourth of the spicy tuna. Garnish with nori powder.

YIELDS 4 SERVINGS

BEEF TARTARE
WITH BRIOCHE TOAST POINTS AND OLIVE OIL

1 pound beef, sirloin strip, tenderloin
2 tablespoons minced shallots
2 tablespoons minced garlic
1 tablespoon mashed anchovies
2 tablespoons Dijon mustard

2 tablespoons chopped capers, rinsed well and
    chopped fine
Maldon salt
Freshly cracked black pepper
Extra virgin olive oil

TOAST POINTS
2 loaves Honey Wheat Brioche (see p. 227)
¼ cup olive oil

The ultimate classic, Beef Tartare is a simple-yet-sophisticated recipe. Here, the homemade toast points of Honey Wheat Brioche, a rich, buttery bread, takes the presentation to the next level. For variety, consider serving the Beef Tartare with a garnish of boiled egg yolk and sliced anchovies.

1.   Place the beef on a cutting board and chop as finely as possible. Place the chopped meat into a bowl and refrigerate until well chilled.
2.   In a mixing bowl, combine shallots, garlic, anchovies, mustard and capers.
3.   Incorporate evenly and fold in chopped beef.

4.   Season with the Maldon salt and pepper to taste.
5.   On four serving plates, place 3 quenelles of beef tartare. Place a Toast Point next to each quenelle using the meat to hold the toast upright. Drizzle olive oil over the tartare and finish with a sprinkle of the Maldon salt.

FOR THE TOAST POINTS:
1.   Preheat oven to 325 degrees.
2.   Slice the brioche 1/4 inch thick. Place bread slices on a sheet pan greased with half the olive oil. Brush remaining oil over the top of the bread.
Bake the brioche for 6 minutes, or until golden brown.

YIELDS 4 SERVINGS

HAMIACHI WITH CUCUMBER NOODLES,
ARUGULA, YUZU SOY AND PINK PEPPERCORN

1 pound hamiachi fillet, skinned and cleaned of
    dark spots
½ cup julienned cucumbers (medium blade
    Japanese mandoline)
¼ cup baby arugula

¼ cup Yuzu Soy
½ tablespoon crushed pink peppercorns
2 tablespoons extra virgin olive oil

YUZU SOY
¼ cup soy
3 tablespoons mirin
2 tablespoons yuzu juice
2 tablespoons fish sauce

Sushi-grade Hamiachi (also known as Yellowtail or Rainbow Runner) with a pop of soy and pink peppercorn makes for a light start to warm weather meals. As always, quality is key when working with raw protein; keep your fish ice-block cold and work quickly to ensure freshness.

1.   Slice hamiachi into 1/8-inch slices, getting as many slices as you can.

2.   In a mixing bowl, toss the cucumbers, arugula and Yuzu Soy.
3.   On four serving plates, place equal amounts of cucumber mixture, top with equal slices of hamiachi and finish with crushed pink peppercorns and a drizzle of oil.

FOR THE YUZU SOY:
1.   In a mixing bowl, combine all ingredients.
2.   Chill for 2 hours.

YIELDS 4 SERVINGS

2

{ A P P E T I Z E R S }

the recipes

Oysters and Caviar with Melted Leeks and Chervil

Roasted Oysters with Green Tomato–Wasabi Cocktail Sauce and Ginger-Soy Butter

Crab Cakes with Truffle Essence Arugula and Sweet Corn Purée

Seared Foie Gras with Spiced Peaches and Corn Muffins

Salt-Cured Foie Gras

Duck Confit and Foie Gras with Leeks, Mizuna and Ginger-Cherry Compote

Beef Spring Rolls

Wok-Seared Squid with Chili Soy and Shiso

Scallops and Braised Bacon with Succotash and Smoked Pork Reduction

Avocado and Soft-shell Crab Roll with Black Spanish Radish and Black Bean Soy

Steamed Squash Blossoms with Ginger Pork and Chanterelles

Benne Seed Shrimp

Butter-Poached Lobster with Truffle Grits Cake and Lobster Glaçage

Lobster "BLT" with Braised Bacon, Lobster Claw, Heirloom Tomato and Garlic Aioli

he conception of appetizers is perhaps my favorite aspect of preparing a menu. Appetizers allow for playful creativity, but at the same time pose a challenge to successfully utilize small amounts of (sometimes precious) ingredients. When you consider that the final dish will be consumed in only a few bites, you have to be on your best game. Cypress's appetizers cover the classic heavyweights such as Foie Gras, and Oysters and Caviar, along with our special interpretations of Asian and Southern influences, as in the popular Tempura Fried Benne Seed Shrimp. My Butter-Poached Lobster with Truffle Grits is a fun take on Charleston's ubiquitous shrimp and grits.

With all of the temptations on the Cypress starter menu, it is not uncommon for people to order two appetizers (to share or savor). Take this into consideration in your own kitchen; choose a few of these recipes to serve in small bites during a cocktail party, or even as a tapas-like light meal for friends. Guests at the restaurant have come to expect unique flavors and presentations in our appetizer offerings and the recipes that follow will not disappoint!

OYSTERS AND CAVIAR
WITH MELTED LEEKS AND CHERVIL

MELTED LEEKS

2 tablespoons water

½ cup leeks, washed and thinly sliced

¼ cup butter

Salt

White pepper

OYSTERS AND CAVIAR

12 west coast oysters (Hood Canal, Steamboat, Naked Roy's Beach)

Beurre Fondue (see p. 113)

1 ounce caviar (American sturgeon, sevruga, osetra)

1 cup rock salt

Fresh chervil

The distinctive contrast of salty caviar and creamy oysters makes this a truly special dish. Buttery "melted" leeks add richness and make a lovely presentation nestled in the bottom of the oyster shell.

FOR THE LEEKS:

1. In a small saucepan, over medium heat, combine water and leeks. Sweat the leeks until the moisture has evaporated. Reduce heat to low and slowly stir in butter.

2. Season with salt and pepper to taste and keep warm.

FOR THE OYSTERS AND CAVIAR:

1. Using an oyster knife, remove top shell of oyster; detach the bottom of the oyster, leaving it in the half shell. Check the oyster for any shell or grit. If there is excess grit, rinse with saltwater; otherwise, place oysters in a small container. Save the cup-shaped oyster shell.

2. Add the shucked oysters to the warm Beurre Monte and poach for 5 minutes.

3. On each of four serving plates, place 1/4 cup rock salt. Place 3 oyster shells on top of the rock salt. Add 1 tablespoon Melted Leeks to each oyster shell. Top with the poached oysters. Add equal amounts of caviar to the top of each oyster. Garnish with fresh chervil sprigs.

YIELDS 4 SERVINGS

ROASTED OYSTERS
WITH GREEN TOMATO–WASABI COCKTAIL SAUCE AND GINGER-SOY BUTTER

GREEN TOMATO–WASABI COCKTAIL SAUCE
1 cup green tomatoes, blanched, peeled and
   small dice
3 tablespoons sugar
3 tablespoons rice wine vinegar
2 teaspoons salt
2 tablespoons wasabi powder

3 tablespoons water
1 tablespoon grated fresh ginger
1 tablespoon chopped cilantro

GINGER-SOY BUTTER
½ cup soy sauce
3 tablespoons fresh grated ginger

3 tablespoons sugar
1 tablespoon chopped cilantro
4 ounces cold butter, cut into pieces

ROASTED OYSTERS
12 large oysters

Outdoor roasts over an open fire are common during oyster season in the lowcountry, and this method of preparation—using the bamboo steamer—allows us to enjoy them throughout the year. The Green Tomato-Wasabi Cocktail Sauce is unique to Cypress and showcases the marriage of our Southern heritage and Asian influences. Green tomato concassé mixes well with the spicy wasabi, while fresh grated ginger gives the sauce a fluid flavor.

FOR THE GREEN TOMATO-WASABI COCKTAIL SAUCE:
1. In a small nonreactive saucepan, combine the tomatoes, sugar, vinegar and salt.
2. Place saucepan over medium-high heat and simmer for 3 to 4 minutes, or until the tomatoes start to break down.
3. Combine the wasabi and water to form a paste, making sure there are no lumps in the mixture.
4. Add wasabi paste and ginger to the tomatoes and cook over medium heat for 2 minutes.
5. Remove from heat and allow mixture to cool completely. When cool, add the cilantro and refrigerate.

FOR THE GINGER-SOY BUTTER:
1. In a small saucepan, combine the soy, ginger, sugar and cilantro. Place the saucepan over medium-high heat and reduce liquid by half.
2. Drop the temperature to low and slowly stir in the cold butter, piece by piece.
3. Strain the butter and keep in a warm location.

FOR THE OYSTERS:
1. Place the oysters in a bamboo steamer; you will probably need to use both baskets.
2. Place the steamer over a pot of boiling water, making sure the pot is wider than the bamboo basket and only has a half inch of water in it.
3. Steam the oysters for 4 minutes and check to see if they have started to open; if not, steam another minute or two.
4. When they start to open, remove from heat. Using a dry towel and an oyster knife, remove the top of the oyster. (The top of the oyster is flat, not cup shaped.) Using the oyster knife, detach the oyster from the bottom and leave it in the shell. Repeat with the remaining oysters.
5. On four serving plates, place 3 oysters and a ramekin of each of the sauces.

YIELDS 4 SERVINGS

CRAB CAKES
WITH TRUFFLE ESSENCE ARUGULA AND SWEET CORN PURÉE

1 egg yolk

3 ounces cream cheese

1 tablespoon chopped scallions

2 teaspoons chopped basil

1 tablespoon lemon juice

½ tablespoon salt

1 teaspoon white pepper

1 dash cayenne pepper

1 pound jumbo lump crabmeat (picked through for shells)

½ cup panko (breadcrumbs)

¼ cup canola oil

2 tablespoons butter

Basil Oil (see p. 24)

SWEET CORN PURÉE

2 tablespoons butter

1½ cups corn kernels

¼ cup minced onion

¼ cup minced celery

1½ cups Corn Stock (see p. 32)

2 teaspoons salt

1 teaspoon white pepper

2 tablespoons butter

TRUFFLE ESSENCE ARUGULA

1 tablespoon chopped garlic

1 tablespoon chopped shallots

¼ cup champagne vinegar

1 tablespoon chopped truffles

2 teaspoons honey

1 teaspoon salt

Pinch of white pepper

¼ cup olive oil

8 ounces arugula, washed and refrigerated

At Cypress, we prepare our popular crab cakes "Maryland-style," with fresh lump crabmeat. Peppery arugula is a foil to the rich truffle and butter flavors of the dish. We serve our crab cakes year-round, but our local season for corn and crabs peaks in the late summer.

It is possible to make the crab cake mixture a day ahead, portion and refrigerate on a sheet pan. The recipe makes 8 cakes as an appetizer or 16 small cakes for party hors d'oeuvres.

1. In a mixing bowl, whip egg yolk and cream cheese until smooth. Add scallions, basil, lemon juice, salt and peppers. Incorporate evenly.
2. Mix in crabmeat carefully, so as not to break up the lumps.
3. Portion crab mixture into 8 equal size cakes.
4. In a separate mixing bowl, place the panko. Coat the crab cakes with the panko.
5. Place a medium-size sauté pan over medium heat. Add oil and butter.
6. Add crab cakes to the pan and sear until golden brown, approximately 3 minutes.
7. Flip crab cakes and cook for another 3 minutes.
8. Remove crab cakes from the pan and place on paper towels to absorb grease.
9. On four serving plates, place Corn Purée and equal amounts of Truffle Essence Arugula. Top with 2 seared crab cakes. Drizzle Basil Oil to garnish.

FOR THE SWEET CORN PUREE:

1. Place a medium-size saucepan over medium heat. Add butter, corn, onion and celery. Sauté until the onion is translucent.
2. Add stock, salt and pepper and cook for 5 minutes. If liquid starts to boil, lower heat.
3. Remove mixture from heat and purée with an immersion blender. Add the last 2 tablespoons of butter and purée until smooth.
4. Strain corn purée and keep warm.

FOR THE TRUFFLE ESSENCE ARUGULA:

1. In a mixing bowl, combine garlic, shallots and vinegar. Allow to sit for 10 minutes.
2. Add truffles, honey, salt, pepper and olive oil. Incorporate evenly.
3. Mix arugula and vinaigrette directly before serving.

YIELDS 4 SERVINGS

SEARED FOIE GRAS
WITH SPICED PEACHES AND CORN MUFFINS

SPICED PEACHES

1 cinnamon stick

1 star anise

3 crushed Szechwan peppercorns

½ cup mirin

2 tablespoons rice wine vinegar

¼ cup sugar

1 teaspoon salt

2 tablespoons butter

2 peaches, peeled, sliced in half and pitted

CORN MUFFINS (YIELDS 1 DOZEN)

¾ cup yellow cornmeal

⅔ cup all-purpose flour

1 teaspoon baking powder

¼ teaspoon salt

3 tablespoons granulated sugar

2 large eggs

¾ cup buttermilk

Canola oil for preparing the pans

2 tablespoons melted butter (keep warm)

Coarse sea salt, as desired

FOR THE SPICED PEACHES:

1. Place the cinnamon stick, star anise and peppercorns in a spice grinder and pulse four times.

2. In a small mixing bowl, combine the mirin, vinegar, sugar, salt and ground spices. Incorporate evenly.

3. Place a sauté pan over high heat. Add the butter and peach halves to the pan and caramelize 3 minutes. Flip the peaches over and add the spice syrup.

4. Cook for 2 minutes. The syrup should lightly caramelize. Remove from heat and keep warm.

FOR THE CORN MUFFINS:

1. Heat cast-iron mini muffin pans in a 425-degree oven for 10 minutes.

2. In a large bowl, stir together the cornmeal, flour, baking powder, salt and sugar.

3. In a separate bowl, lightly whip together the eggs and buttermilk.

4. Carefully remove the hot pans from the oven. Brush the cups of the pans with canola oil. Be sure to remove any excess oil that pools in the bottom of the cups.

5. Stir buttermilk mixture into the combined dry ingredients. Add the warm, melted butter to the batter and stir until just combined.

6. Divide the batter into muffin cups. The batter should fill the cups no more than three-fourths full.

7. Sprinkle the tops of each muffin with as much coarse sea salt as desired.

8. Bake for 10 to 15 minutes, or until the muffins are golden on top and done throughout. A skewer or toothpick inserted into the center of a muffin should come out clean, with no wet batter clinging to it.

9. Remove the pans from the oven and immediately unmold the muffins by inverting the pans over a clean countertop. If your muffins stick, turn the pans right side up, run a knife with a thin blade between each muffin and their cup. Be sure to use the cast iron as your guide, putting pressure on the metal and away from the muffin as you slide the knife around the cup. If your knife does not stay in contact with the muffin pan, you will slice into your muffins. Invert the pan again and give a gentle tap or two to release any stubborn muffins.

Continued on next page

SEARED FOIE GRAS
4 slices Salt-Cured Foie Fras (see next page)
White pepper

FOR THE SEARED FOIE GRAS:

1. Season the foie gras slices with a light dusting of white pepper on both sides.

2. Place a sauté pan over high heat. When hot, add the sliced foie gras to the pan, **[1]**. Cook for 1 1/2 minutes while basting the slices with the fat that comes off of them, **[2]**.

3. Flip and repeat on other side, **[3]**.

4. Remove foie gras from pan and place on paper towels to absorb grease, **[4]**.

5. On four serving plates, place a Spiced Peach half and equal amounts of syrup in the middle of the plate. Place a slice of foie gras on top of the peach half and a Corn Muffin next to this.

SALT-CURED FOIE GRAS

1 lobe foie gras (about 1½ to 2 pounds)
3 pounds salt

Foie gras is not an ingredient for the lighthearted cook. It is expensive (about 35 to 40 dollars per pound) and difficult to clean. It should be treated as a special product—perhaps to challenge your culinary skill and/or impress guests. If you are prepared for the undertaking, foie gras will produce great reward in its unmatched taste. This salt-cured version adds flavor and extracts moisture, producing a delicious caramel crust when seared.

FOR THE FOIE GRAS:

1. Allow the foie gras to come to room temperature. It will resemble the texture of soft clay, **[1]**.

2. Separate the lobe by following the seam in the middle and pull apart. Remove and discard the white, fatty membrane in the middle, **[2]**.

3. Place a sharp knife in hot water and slice the foie gras into 1-inch-thick slices. You should end up with 6 to 8 equal-size pieces, **[3]**.

4. In a baking dish, place half the salt.

5. Cut a piece of cheesecloth twice the size of your baking dish. Place the foie gras on the cheesecloth, **[4]**. Cover with a single layer of cheesecloth.

6. Cover with the remaining salt, **[5] [6]**.

7. Wrap tightly with plastic wrap and refrigerate for 18 hours. Do not forget about it; it will become too salty if left too long.

8. Remove the foie gras from the salt, brushing off any excess.

The foie gras is now ready for use or can be frozen for 3 weeks.

YIELDS 6-8 SERVINGS

DUCK CONFIT AND FOIE GRAS
WITH LEEKS, MIZUNA AND GINGER-CHERRY COMPOTE

DUCK LEGS

¼ cup salt

¼ cup sugar

½ tablespoon sage leaves

½ tablespoon thyme leaves

1 teaspoon white pepper

1 teaspoon orange zest

2 duck legs (trim off excess fat and save)

2 to 3 cups duck fat

GINGER-CHERRY COMPOTE

½ cup sun-dried cherries

¼ cup ginger, fine dice

¼ cup sugar

1 teaspoon salt

¼ cup rice wine vinegar

2 tablespoons finely sliced chives

DUCK CONFIT AND FOIE GRAS

2 Duck Legs (see left)

2 tablespoons butter

4 ounces shiitake mushrooms

½ cup leeks, washed and cut in ¼-inch half moons

6 ounces mizuna

4 slices Salt-Cured Foie Gras (see p. 61)

White pepper

This is a delicious hot salad for fall. The ingredients are decadent and their sweet and savory flavors play well together.

FOR THE DUCK LEGS:

1. In a spice grinder, combine salt, sugar, sage, thyme, pepper and orange zest. Grind to fine mixture.

2. Rub only the meaty part of the legs with some of the salt mixture. Place the legs in a baking pan, fat side down. Wrap tightly and refrigerate for 24 hours.

3. Preheat oven to 220 degrees.

4. Remove the duck legs and rinse with water to remove all salt.

5. Pat the duck legs completely dry with kitchen towels.

6. Place duck legs in a roasting pan just large enough to hold them, meat side down.

7. Place duck fat in a pan and liquefy.

8. Cover duck legs with warm duck fat.

9. Place a tight fitting lid on the roasting pan. If you don't have one, use aluminum foil.

10. Cook at 220 degrees for 5 hours.

11. Remove duck from pan and place on kitchen towels to absorb fat.

12. Place the duck legs in a container with a tight fitting lid and cover with duck fat.

13. Make sure not to get any liquids other than fat in this container. Place container in refrigerator. Will keep for several weeks.

FOR GINGER-CHERRY COMPOTE:

1. In a small saucepan, combine cherries, ginger, sugar, salt and vinegar. Place over medium heat and reduce by one-fourth.

2. Set aside and keep warm.

3. Directly before serving, stir in chives.

FOR THE DUCK CONFIT AND FOIE GRAS:

1. Pull meat off duck legs. Discard fat and bones.

2. Place sauté pan over medium-high heat. Add butter to pan.

3. When butter is melted, add shiitake mushrooms. Cook for 2 minutes. Mushrooms will be lightly caramelized.

4. Drop temperature to medium-low. Add leeks and duck confit. Cook for 4 minutes, stirring occasionally to keep from sticking.

5. Remove pan from heat and keep warm.

6. Add mizuna just before serving.

7. Season the foie gras slices with a light dusting of white pepper on both sides.

8. Place a sauté pan over high heat. When hot, add the sliced foie gras to the pan. Cook for 1 1/2 minutes while basting the slices with the fat that comes off of them. Flip and repeat on other side.

9. Remove foie gras from pan and place on paper towels to absorb fat.

10. On four serving plates, place equal amounts of the warm duck salad in the middle.

11. Top with a piece of foie gras. Place 1 tablespoon of the Ginger-Cherry Compote on top of each piece of foie gras. Drizzle remaining syrup around plate.

YIELDS 4 SERVINGS

BEEF SPRING ROLLS

1 pound beef tenderloin tips, minced fine
½ cup fish sauce
2 tablespoons sambal oelek
½ tablespoon chopped cilantro

½ tablespoon chopped mint
¼ cup chopped scallions
12 spring roll wrappers
1 egg, beaten

1 gallon peanut or canola oil
Sea salt
½ cup Sour Soy Vinaigrette (see p. 97)

This fragrant appetizer is good on its own, but I recommend that you add Sour Soy dipping sauce for an extra punch of flavor. Wrapping the rolls is somewhat of an art form, but not impossible.

In a mixing bowl, combine beef, fish sauce, sambal, cilantro, mint and scallions.

1. Incorporate mixture evenly and divide into 12 equal portions. Lay the spring roll wrappers on a table with each facing you like a diamond. Place one portion of beef on each wrapper on the corner closest to you, **[1]**.

2. Roll the beef, pressing tightly until you get halfway, **[2]**. Fold the sides in, **[3]**, and continue to roll forward, **[4]**. Brush with beaten egg on the last corner, **[5]**.

3. In a large pot, heat the oil to 350 degrees. Fry the spring rolls until golden brown (approximately 4 minutes). Remove the rolls from the oil and place in a bowl with paper towels to absorb excess oil, **[6]**. Season with sea salt.

4. On four serving plates, place 3 spring rolls. Place equal amounts of Sour Soy Vinaigrette in four ramekins and serve with the spring rolls.

YIELDS 4 SERVINGS

WOK-SEARED SQUID
WITH CHILI SOY AND SHISO

1½ pounds squid tubes and tentacles
3 tablespoons canola oil
¼ cup minced ginger

¼ cup minced shallots
¼ cup fish sauce
¼ cup Chili Soy (see p. 22)
1 tablespoon chopped shiso (can substitute basil)

1 tablespoon chopped cilantro
2 tablespoons butter
Mint Oil (see p. 24)

Speed and organization are key with this dish, as the squid can overcook and become rubbery. Have your mise en place (ingredients list) lined up and ready to go when the wok is smoking hot. If your stove is not set up for a wok, a large sauté pan will also work; just be sure that the pan is heating evenly. The recipe is set up for a large sauté pan.

1. Clean the squid, making sure there are no beaks or cartilage. Beaks are found in the center of the tentacles; remove with a paring knife. Cartilage is found in the tubes and can be removed by hand.
2. Cut the tubes in half, lengthwise, and slice on a bias. Do not cut the tentacles.
3. Place a large, heavy-bottomed sauté pan over high heat. Let the pan get smoking hot.

4. Add the oil, ginger and shallots to the sauté pan. Keep the pan moving or stir with a wooden spoon to prevent burning.
5. Add the squid tubes and tentacles to the sauté pan and sear quickly. The cooking time is very short; the squid will begin to curl.
6. Add the fish sauce and Chili Soy to the sauté pan. Liquid will reduce by half quickly and become syrup consistency. Remove sauté pan from heat.
7. Add shiso, cilantro and the butter to the sauté pan and incorporate evenly.
8. On four serving plates, place equal amounts of the squid and sauce.
9. Garnish with a drizzle of Mint Oil.

YIELDS 4 SERVINGS

SCALLOPS AND BRAISED BACON
WITH SUCCOTASH AND SMOKED PORK REDUCTION

BRAISED BACON
1 cup water
½ cup salt
¼ cup sugar
1 teaspoon sel rose (curing salt)
1 bulb garlic, split in half
4 sprigs thyme
1 teaspoon white peppercorns

½ gallon ice water
2 pounds fresh pork bellies, skin removed
¼ cup canola oil
2 cups Smoked Pork Stock (see p. 34)
2 cups water
Salt and pepper
Succotash Fricassee (see p. 202)
Salt

White pepper
canola oil
4 large dry-pack scallops (U-10)
¼ cup canola oil
Coarse sea salt
Chive tips
Chive Oil (see p. 24)

If you like bacon, you will love my braised pork belly. Money back guarantee. We use Kurobuto pork, which is from Berkshire Pork (raised at Snake River Farms in Texas); it's the Kobe beef of pork. I use this in a braising recipe because it is inter-muscularly marbleized, i. e. yielding more meat and less fat. Pressed bellies are taken out of the braise so that they are firm, then seared for crunch and soft on the inside. The contrast of textures and intense flavor is unique.

FOR THE BRAISED BACON:

1. In a pot, combine 1 cup of water, salt, sugar and sel rose and bring to a boil.
2. Add the garlic, thyme and peppercorns to the pot and remove from heat. Add the ice water and stir until cold.
3. Add the fresh pork belly to the liquid and place in the refrigerator for 1 day.
4. Preheat oven to 250 degrees.
5. Remove the pork from the liquid and pat dry with kitchen towels.
6. Place a pot over medium-high heat and add the oil. Let the oil get hot.
7. Add the pork belly to the pan, meat side down, and sear for 5 minutes. Meat will have a crispy crust. Carefully flip the pork and cook for another five minutes.
8. Remove the pan from heat and add the smoked pork stock and water. This should cover the pork belly by a little more than half.
9. Cover pot with a tight lid or aluminum foil. Place in oven and cook for 6 hours.
10. When pork belly is done, remove from oven and allow to cool in the pot. When cool, refrigerate for a least one full day.
11. Discard any solidified fat from the pot. Remove the pork belly from the pot and place on a cutting board.

12. Place the pot back on the stove and bring to a simmer. Skim off any fat or scum that rises to the surface. Reduce the stock by half and adjust seasoning with salt and pepper. Strain the stock and keep warm.
13. Cut the braised pork belly into four equal size pieces.

FOR THE ASSEMBLY:

1. Make the succotash and keep warm.
2. Season the braised pork with salt and pepper on both sides.
3. Place a sauté pan over medium high heat and add a thin layer of canola oil. Let the oil get hot and add the braised bacon.
4. Cook the bacon for 2 minutes on the first side; bacon should have a crispy golden crust. Flip the bacon over and cook another 2 minutes. Remove bacon from pan and place on kitchen towels to absorb excess fat.
5. Place the scallops on kitchen towels to dry off excess moisture.
6. Season the scallops with salt and pepper.
7. Place a large sauté pan over medium-high heat. Add the 1/4 cup canola oil to the pan and sear the scallops 1 1/2 minutes. Flip and sear other side 1 1/2 minutes. Remove from pan and place on kitchen towels.
8. Remove bacon from the oven and place on kitchen towels to absorb fat.
9. On four serving plates, place equal amounts of the smoked pork reduction. Place equal amounts of the succotash on top of the sauce. Top with a seared scallop and a block of braised bacon. Garnish with a sprinkle of coarse sea salt, a chive tip and a drizzle of Chive Oil.

YIELDS 4 SERVINGS

AVOCADO AND SOFT-SHELL CRAB ROLL
WITH BLACK SPANISH RADISH AND BLACK BEAN SOY

1 gallon peanut or canola oil
2 scallions (green tops only)
1 black Spanish radish (can substitute
   daikon radish)

1 avocado, peeled, pitted and cut into quarters
4 soft-shell crabs
Tempura Batter (see p. 133)

Fine sea salt
Black Bean Soy (see p. 22)

Come soft-shell crab season in Charleston (April and early September), this variation of a sushi roll can be found on Cypress's appetizer specials.

1. Place oil in a large pot. Attach a thermometer to the side of the pot and heat oil to 350 degrees.
2. Cut scallion tops into 2-inch lengths. Julienne tops thinly and place in cold water. The scallions will curl as they get cold. Using a mandolin or a chiba slicer, slice radish into long, paper-thin strips. You will need at least 8 slices. Soak the slices in water.
3. Place the avocado quarters on a cutting board and slice into strips, lengthwise.
4. Clean the soft-shell crabs using kitchen shears. Cut off the face by half an inch. Remove the lungs on both sides by pulling up on each side of the top shell and cutting them out. Remove the skirt on the bottom of the crab. Press the stomach and calcium deposits out of the crab through the opening where the face was removed.

5. Place the soft-shell crabs on paper towels and then press them dry. Keep refrigerated until ready to use.
6. Line a small bowl with paper towels.
7. Holding the hind legs, dip crabs in tempura batter and carefully add to hot oil. Be sure not to overcrowd the pan. You may need to cook in 2 batches. Cook for 2 1/2 to 3 minutes, flipping the crabs as needed.
8. Remove crabs from oil and place in a bowl with paper towels to absorb excess oil. Season with fine sea salt.
9. Lay the radish slices in groups of two and place the avocado in the middle, [1]. Lay the crabs on top and roll tightly, [2] [3].
10. Cut the rolled soft-shell crabs in half.
11. On four serving plates, place 2 tablespoons Black Bean Soy in the center of each plate. Place the rolls, one on top of the other, over the Black Bean Soy. Garnish with scallion curls.

YIELDS 4 SERVINGS

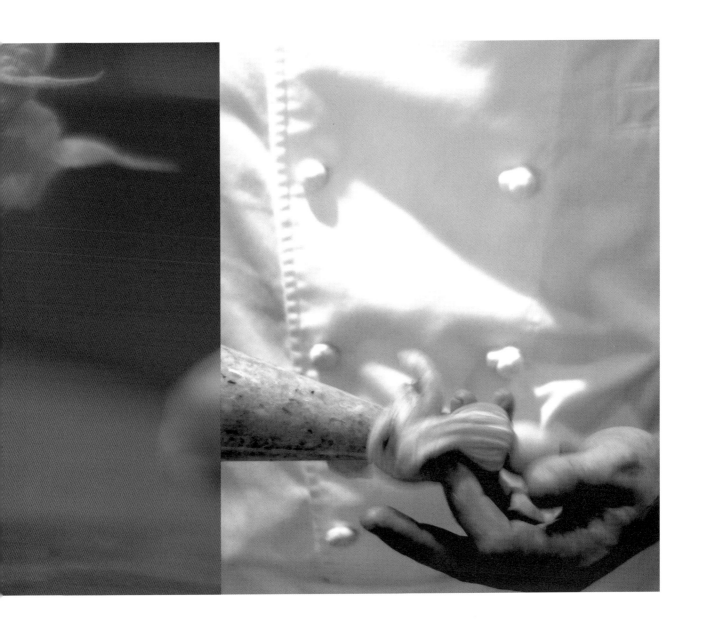

STEAMED SQUASH BLOSSOMS
WITH GINGER PORK AND CHANTERELLES

½ pound ground pork
¼ cup mirin
½ tablespoon chopped garlic
1 tablespoon chopped ginger
½ tablespoon chopped cilantro

½ tablespoon lemon grass
1 tablespoon salt
1 teaspoon white pepper
8 squash blossoms (fruit attached)
2 tablespoons olive oil

½ pound chanterelles
1 teaspoon salt
½ teaspoon white pepper
2 tablespoons Aged Balsamic

Fresh squash blossoms signal the peak of spring and arrival of summer in the lowcountry. This dish brings the delicate blossoms into focus with light Asian notes of ginger and lemongrass. A balsamic reduction and chanterelle mushrooms (also a local springtime delicacy) add an earthy counterpoint.

1. In a mixing bowl, combine all ingredients except squash blossoms and incorporate evenly.
2. Place mixture into a piping bag.
3. Pipe mixture into the squash blossoms, [1].
4. Place squash blossoms into a bamboo steamer and steam for 4 to 5 minutes, [2].
5. Place a sauté pan on high heat and add olive oil.
6. Add chanterelles to the sauté pan and keep enough space between them so that they caramelize evenly.
7. When caramelized, flip the chanterelles, [3], and then season with salt and pepper.
8. Lay the chanterelles on paper towels to absorb oil.
9. To plate the blossoms, place equal amounts of chanterelles in the center of a serving plate.
10. On top the chanterelles, place 2 steamed squash blossoms. Place 1/2 tablespoon Aged Balsamic around the plate.

YIELDS 4 SERVINGS

CHEF DEIHL'S NOTE: If you cannot find ground pork at your local meat counter, purchase pork shoulder or fatty nuggets of pork and work the meat through a meat grinder. A food processor will also cut the pork down to the appropriate texture.

BENNE SEED SHRIMP

1 pound shrimp, peeled and deveined

1 cup cornstarch

1 cup all-purpose flour

3 tablespoons black sesame seeds

3 tablespoons white sesame seeds

1½ cups cold soda water

½ gallon peanut or canola oil

1 tablespoon fine sea salt

¼ cup Chili Glaze (see p. 22)

This sweet and spicy tempura appetizer has been on Cypress's menu since the start. The shrimp may be served on a platter as hors d'oeuvres for guests at home. Be sure to fry extras—they never last long!

1. Place the shrimp on paper towels to keep them dry. The drier the shrimp, the crispier the batter. Keep refrigerated until ready to use.

2. In a medium-size mixing bowl, combine cornstarch, flour, sesame seeds and cold soda water; whip until incorporated.

3. Keep cold until ready to use.

4. Place oil in large saucepan. Attach a thermometer to the side of the pan and heat oil to 350 degrees.

5. Line a small bowl with paper towels.

6. Dip shrimp in benne seed batter and carefully add to hot oil. Be sure not to overcrowd the pan. You may need to cook in multiple batches. Cook for 2 1/2 to 3 minutes, flipping the shrimp as needed.

7. Remove shrimp from oil and place in bowl with paper towels to absorb excess oil. Season with fine sea salt.

8. On four serving plates, place equal amounts of shrimp and drizzle Chili Glaze around shrimp.

YIELDS 4 SERVINGS

BUTTER-POACHED LOBSTER
WITH TRUFFLE GRITS CAKE AND LOBSTER GLAÇAGE

4 Truffle Grits Cakes (see p. 137)
2 (1¼-pound) lobsters (see Lobster Cooking
    Process p. 79)
Beurre Fondue (see p. 113)
1 egg white
¼ cup white cornmeal

Canola oil
Salt
White pepper
Tarragon leaves

LOBSTER GLAÇAGE
1 cup Shellfish Stock (see p. 35)
2 tablespoons heavy cream

2 egg yolks
3 tablespoons water
1 tablespoon lemon juice
¾ cup Clarified Butter, warm to touch (see p. 26)
Salt
White pepper

1. Cook the truffle grits and cut into circles as directed.
2. Cook and clean the lobsters as described.
3. Make the Beurre Fondue and keep over low heat. Add the lobster meat to the beurre fondue and poach for 5 minutes.
4. Make the Lobster Glaçage and keep warm.
5. Place the egg white in a small bowl and lightly beat. Place the cornmeal on a plate.
6. Brush the egg whites on both sides of the grits cake and coat each side with cornmeal. Repeat with the remaining grits cakes.
7. Place a sauté pan over medium heat and add a thin layer of canola oil. When the oil is hot, add the grits cakes and cook for 4 minutes. Flip the cakes over and cook for another 4 minutes. Remove from pan, place on paper towels and serve while crispy.
8. Remove the lobster from the Beurre Fondue and place on paper towels to absorb excess butter. Slice the lobster tails in half. Season all meat with salt and white pepper.
9. On four serving plates, place a tablespoon of the Lobster Glaçage in the center. Place the Truffle Grits Cakes on top of the glaçage and lightly press down. Place half a tail and one claw on top of the grits cakes. Top with the glaçage and, using a blow torch, brown the glaçage. Garnish with the tarragon leaves.

FOR LOBSTER GLAÇAGE:

1. In a small saucepan add the stock. Place over medium-low heat and reduce by three-fourths. Add the heavy cream and simmer for 2 minutes
2. In a small mixing bowl, combine the egg yolks, water and lemon juice.
3. Place the bowl over a simmering pot of water or place over a low heat flame and whip continuously. The mixture will double in volume and will start to steam. Steam is good; it is the water cooking out.
4. The eggs will become tight as they cook. When they are fully cooked you will see ribbons form after the whisk moves through the eggs. The eggs should taste cooked when done.
5. Remove the bowl from heat and place on a towel to keep the bowl from moving.
6. Slowly add the warm butter in a thin stream while whipping continuously. Continue working until all the butter is added. The mixture should be thick and creamy.
7. Add the reduced stock and cream.
8. Season to taste with salt and pepper.
9. Keep in a warm location in a crock or insulated container until needed. But don't leave too long. This sauce is very unstable during changes in temperature.

YIELDS 4 SERVINGS

lobster cooking process

3 gallons water
½ cup salt
2 (1¼-pound) lobsters

1. Place a large pot containing water and salt over high heat. Bring to a boil.
2. Using a sharp knife, pierce the lobster on the bottom side of the head between the eyes. This will kill the lobsters.
3. Place the lobsters in a roasting pan and cover with the boiling water, [1].
4. Let sit for 3 minutes.
5. Using rubber gloves, pull the lobsters from the water. Remove the tails and set aside. Remove the arms from the body and add back to the water and allow to sit for another 2 minutes.
6. Remove the tail meat from the shell by removing the fan and pulling the shell away from the tail, [2]. Using a wooden skewer, remove the vein from the tail, [3].
7. Remove the claws from the water and separate claws from knuckles.
8. Remove pincher from claw, trying to remove the feather along with the pincher.
9. Using a heavy knife, crack the top of the claw and remove meat, [4].
10. Using kitchen shears, cut through knuckles and remove meat.
11. Place lobster meat, [5], in containers to refrigerate or use immediately.

LOBSTER "BLT" WITH BRAISED BACON,
LOBSTER CLAW, HEIRLOOM TOMATO AND GARLIC AIOLI

Beurre Fondue (see p. 113)
4 lobster claws (see Lobster Cooking Process
    p. 79)
4 blocks Braised Bacon (see p. 69)

Salt
White pepper
Canola oil
2 loaves Honey Wheat Brioche (see p. 227)

1 tablespoon extra virgin olive oil
1 heirloom tomato
Roasted Garlic Aioli (see p. 91)
1 head frisee, washed (tender center yellow
    leaves only)

This is a decadent upscale version of one of the South's favorite sandwiches. I typically prepare it for our private dining groups, or as a special addition to the New Year's Eve menu.

1. Make the Beurre Fondue and keep over low heat. Add the lobster claws and poach for 5 minutes.
2. Season the braised pork with salt and pepper on both sides.
3. Place a sauté pan over medium-high heat and add a thin layer of canola oil. Let the oil get hot and add the braised bacon.
4. Cook the bacon for 2 minutes on the first side; bacon should have a crispy golden crust. Flip the bacon over and cook another 2 minutes. Remove from pan and place on paper towels to absorb excess fat.
5. Slice the brioche into four 1-inch-thick slices and toast.
6. Cut the heirloom tomato into a square the same size as the brioche and slice into blocks. Rub the tomatoes with olive oil and season with salt and pepper.
7. On four serving plates, place 1/2 tablespoon Roasted Garlic Aioli in the center. Stack the toast, tomato, bacon and lobster and garnish with the frisée.

YIELDS 4 SERVINGS

{ S A L A D S   A N D   C H E E S E }

3

the recipes

Arugula Salad with Walnut Vinaigrette, Goat Cheese
and Toasted Walnuts

Almond-Fried Goat Brie with Cranberry-Walnut
Chutney and Bitter Greens

Salad Niçoise with Summer Beans, Black Olive Oil
and Roasted Garlic Aioli

Seared Duck and Watercress with Feta, Dried Figs
and Balsamic Syrup

Cypress Caesar Salad

Garden and Herb Salad with Garlic Shallot
Vinaigrette

Asian Beef Salad with Sour Soy Vinaigrette

Fromage Blanc with Dried Fig Compote, Watercress
and Aged Balsamic

Portobello Mille-Feulle with Boursin Cheese,
Spinach and Port Wine Syrup

Thai Seafood Salad

As both starters and bookends for many meals, salads and cheese can rev up one's appetite or pro-vide respite for the palate, depending on their placement. Personally, I prefer the salad after a raw course to lead into an appetizer and then the main entrée. Alternating between heavy and light foods makes for a balanced presentation and enjoyment of each course without feeling too full.

When designing a salad, I take into consideration what each season offers in the way of fresh vege-tables, fruits and herbs. Choose your own combinations wisely as it's important that ingredients com-plement one another to provide your hot, sour, salty and sweet flavor profiles. For a summertime composition, I often toss watermelon, arugula and watercress finished with Feta cheese. This mix of sweet and peppery flavors plays well with the heat. For winter, buttery lettuces graced with crisp apples and pears are divine sprinkled with toasted nuts, goat cheese and a drizzle of Balsamic vine-gar and olive oil.

Cypress's signature Caesar Salad can easily be made and prepared, as in the restaurant, tableside at home. This adds entertainment to the most simple roast chicken meal, and the fresh flavor of our homemade Caesar dressing cannot be beat.

ARUGULA SALAD WITH WALNUT VINAIGRETTE,
GOAT CHEESE AND TOASTED WALNUTS

TOASTED WALNUTS

3 tablespoons powdered sugar

1 teaspoon fine sea salt

4 tablespoons water

½ cup walnuts

WALNUT VINAIGRETTE

1 tablespoon Dijon mustard

4 tablespoons walnut vinegar

2 tablespoons sherry vinegar

5 tablespoons walnut oil

1 teaspoon salt

¼ cup rice wine vinegar

2 tablespoons finely sliced chives

ARUGULA SALAD

4 ounces goat cheese

12 ounces arugula, washed

Salt

White pepper

Aged balsamic

Peppery arugula contrasts nicely with the goat cheese and balsamic vinegar in this versatile salad composition. It's also delicious with Gorgonzola or Roquefort cheese. Add sliced pears for a hint of sweetness.

FOR THE TOASTED WALNUTS:

1. Preheat oven to 350 degrees.
2. In a mixing bowl combine the sugar, salt and water. Mix evenly, then add the walnuts and coat evenly.
3. Place the nuts on a sheet pan and bake for 10 minutes.
4. Cool before serving. Store in a sealed container.

FOR THE WALNUT VINAIGRETTE:

In a mixing bowl, combine the mustard and the vinegars. Using a whisk, stir in the oil.

FOR THE ARUGULA SALAD:

1. Place the goat cheese in a piping bag with a medium tip. Let the cheese sit at room temperature for 25 minutes. This will make it easier to pipe the cheese.
2. Place the arugula in a mixing bowl, add the Walnut Vinaigrette and season with salt and pepper to taste. Mix evenly.
3. On four serving plates, pipe a 4-inch ring of goat cheese in the center. Place an equal amount of dressed greens in the middle of the goat cheese circle and drizzle the salad with aged balsamic. Finish with Toasted Walnuts.

YIELDS 4 SERVINGS

ALMOND-FRIED GOAT BRIE
WITH CRANBERRY-WALNUT CHUTNEY AND BITTER GREENS

CRANBERRY-WALNUT CHUTNEY
¼ cup granulated sugar
¼ cup light brown sugar
½ cup cider vinegar
¼ cup dried cranberries
¼ cup walnuts
½ tablespoon orange zest (on microplane)

TOAST POINTS
½ baguette sliced on a bias into four
¼-inch-thick slices
¼ cup olive oil

GARLIC SHALLOT VINAIGRETTE
2 tablespoons diced shallots
2 tablespoons minced garlic
1 tablespoon Dijon mustard
4 tablespoons champagne vinegar
4 tablespoons olive oil

ALMOND-FRIED GOAT BRIE
1 gallon peanut or canola oil
4 pieces goat brie
1 cup all-purpose flour
2 eggs, beaten
¼ cup almond flour
¼ cup panko
½ pound mixed greens, washed
4 ounces frisee (yellow center leaves only)
Salt
White pepper

A Cypress classic, this has been on our menu since the beginning. If you cannot find goat brie, which I prefer for its "grassy" flavor, you may substitute Camembert or domestic saga bleu cheese.

FOR THE CRANBERRY-WALNUT CHUTNEY :
1. In a small saucepan, combine sugars and vinegar and reduce by half. Mixture should become syrupy.
2. Remove from heat. Stir in cranberries, walnuts and orange zest. Allow mixture to cool to room temperature.

FOR THE TOAST POINTS:
1. Preheat oven to 325 degrees.
2. Place bread on a sheet pan greased with the olive oil.
3. Bake toast points for 5 to 6 minutes, or until golden brown.

FOR THE GARLIC SHALLOT VINAIGRETTE:
1. In a mixing bowl, combine shallots, garlic, mustard and champagne vinegar.
2. Using a whisk, stir in olive oil.

FOR THE ALMOND-FRIED GOAT BRIE:
1. In a large pot, heat oil to 350 degrees.
2. Place flour in a small bowl. Place eggs in a separate small bowl. Place almond flour and panko in a third small bowl.
3. Dip the goat brie into the flour, dusting off any excess.
4. Place brie in egg wash and coat evenly.
5. Transfer brie and dredge in almond flour mixture.
6. Place the brie in the hot oil and fry until golden brown (approximately 1 1/2 minutes). Remove from oil. Place on paper towels to absorb oil and keep warm.
7. Toss greens with vinaigrette evenly. Season to taste with salt and pepper.
8. On four serving plates, place equal amounts of greens, 1 toast point and 1 piece fried brie. Put 2 tablespoons Cranberry-Walnut Chutney on top of the brie.

YIELDS 4 SERVINGS

washing lettuce and greens

It is important to wash all of your ingredients—especially lettuces, which tend to have dirt and sand from the fields. If you buy whole heads of lettuce or even pre-washed greens, you still need to wash them. Washing will not only help remove dirt and an occasional bug, but will also allow the lettuce to become crisp and crunchy.

TO WASH LETTUCE AND GREENS:
1. Place salad greens in a large bowl of warm water (no warmer than 90 degrees). Soak the greens for no more than 5 minutes.
2. Pull the greens from the water and place in a salad spinner. Look at the water in the bottom of the bowl. Is there sand and dirt in it?
3. Spin greens slowly; you don't want to bruise the greens. After spinning, place the greens in a bowl with paper towels to absorb excess moisture. Place the bowl, uncovered, in the refrigerator for at least 20 minutes.

If the greens are to be stored for later use, cover them tightly; air will dry them out.

SALAD NIÇOISE WITH SUMMER BEANS,
BLACK OLIVE OIL AND ROASTED GARLIC AIOLI

5 eggs

½ cup waxed beans, blanched

¼ cup dragon beans, blanched

¼ cup romano beans, blanched

¼ cup haricots verts, blanched

8 white anchovies

¼ cup lemon juice

3 tablespoons extra virgin olive oil

Salt

White pepper

1 tablespoon tarragon leaves

1 tablespoon chervil leaves

ROASTED GARLIC AIOLI

3 bulbs garlic

3 tablespoons extra virgin olive oil

1 egg yolk

2 tablespoons white wine vinegar

4 tablespoons water

½ cup canola oil

Salt

White pepper

BLACK OLIVE OIL

3 tablespoons cured black olives

3 tablespoons extra virgin olive oil

This summertime salad showcases fresh farmers market beans. You can create a more substantial salad by adding a piece of grilled tuna or high-quality preserved tuna.

1. In a small saucepan, cover eggs with cold water and place over medium-low heat. Cook for 20 minutes. Test one egg to make sure they will all have a slightly soft center. Shock the eggs in ice water. They will continue to cook as they get cold. (Salt and pepper the tested egg and enjoy!)
2. Slice all the beans on a bias into 1-inch pieces. Combine in a medium-size mixing bowl.
3. Add the anchovies, lemon juice and olive oil. Season with salt and pepper.
4. Before serving, toss in the tarragon and chervil leaves and mix evenly.
5. Slice the eggs in half.
6. On four serving plates, draw a large oval in the center of the plate with 1/2 cup Roasted Garlic Aioli. Place an equal amount of the beans and anchovies in the center of the plate and place the halved eggs outside the beans. Garnish with a drizzle of Black Olive Oil.

FOR THE ROASTED GARLIC AIOLI

1. Preheat oven to 350 degrees.
2. Rub the garlic bulbs with extra virgin olive oil and place on pieces of aluminum foil. Fold the ends in to create a tight package. Place on a sheet pan and bake for 1 hour.
3. Remove from oven and cool completely.
4. When cool, slice the bulbs in half and squeeze out the roasted garlic.
5. In a food processor, combine the garlic, egg yolk, vinegar and water. Purée and slowly stream in the oil. Season with salt and pepper and transfer to a small squirt bottle.
6. Refrigerate for up to 5 days, tightly sealed.

FOR THE BLACK OLIVE OIL

1. Place both ingredients in a spice grinder and purée until smooth.
2. Place oil in a small container. Leave at room temperature and stir well before serving.

YIELDS 4 SERVINGS

SEARED DUCK AND WATERCRESS WITH FETA,
DRIED FIGS AND BALSAMIC SYRUP

¼ cup dried figs, stems removed, split in half
½ cup balsamic vinegar
2 Muscovy duck breasts, 10 to 12 ounces each
Salt
White pepper

4 sprigs thyme
2 cloves garlic, crushed
2 tablespoons butter
8 ounces watercress
¼ cup sherry vinegar

3 tablespoons olive oil
4 ounces feta, cut into four small blocks
Coarse sea salt

Creamy, salty feta cheese from Split Creek Farms in Anderson, South Carolina, balances the sweetness of the figs in this delicious fall salad.

1. In a small saucepan, combine the figs and the balsamic vinegar. Place over medium heat and reduce for 8 minutes. Should be reduced by half and syrupy. Remove from heat and keep warm.

2. Season the duck breasts with salt and pepper on the meat side only.

3. Place a sauté pan over medium heat. Add the duck breasts fat side down to the pan and allow the fat to render and become crispy, 8 to 10 minutes. Flip the breasts over, add the thyme, garlic and butter and cook for 3 minutes, basting with the fat, the herbs and the butter.

4. Remove the duck from the pan and place on paper towels to absorb excess fat. Rest the meat for 4 minutes.

5. In a medium-size bowl, toss the watercress, sherry vinegar and oil. Season with salt and pepper to taste.

6. Slice the duck breast into 1/8-inch slices.

7. On each of four serving plates, place a block of the feta in the middle. Lay equal amounts of watercress on top of the feta. Place equal slices of duck on top of the watercress. Spoon 1 tablespoon of the warm figs on top of the duck and drizzle balsamic syrup around the salad. Finish with a couple grains of the coarse sea salt.

YIELDS 4 SERVINGS

CYPRESS CAESAR SALAD

		GARLIC CROUTONS
2 cloves garlic	6 drops Tabasco	3 cloves garlic
6 anchovy fillets	1 cup olive oil	½ cup olive oil
1½ tablespoons Dijon mustard	1 pound romaine hearts, washed and ribs removed	1 teaspoon salt
2 egg yolks	Salt	½ teaspoon white pepper
1½ tablespoons lemon juice	White pepper	1 baguette
1 tablespoon Worcestershire sauce	3 ounces Parmesan cheese	

1. Using two forks, place garlic and anchovies in a large wooden bowl and crush to a paste, **[1]**.
2. Add the Dijon mustard and mix, making a smooth paste.
3. Add the egg yolks, lemon juice, Worcestershire and Tabasco, **[2-4]**, and incorporate to a creamy paste.
4. Slowly stir in oil while beating vigorously to emulsify the dressing.
5. Incorporate the romaine with the dressing. The greens should be well coated.
6. Season with salt and pepper. Mix evenly.
7. On four serving plates, place equal amounts of romaine and finish with Garlic Croutons. Finish with freshly grated Parmesan, **[5-6]**.

FOR THE GARLIC CROUTONS:
1. Preheat oven to 300 degrees.
2. In a blender, combine the garlic, oil, salt and pepper. Purée until smooth
3. Trim the ends and sides of the baguette to create a long square.
4. Cut the bread into 1/2 inch blocks.
5. Place bread cubes in a mixing bowl and add the puréed garlic. Mix evenly; all blocks should be coated.
6. Place the bread cubes on a sheet pan and bake for 15 minutes. Croutons should be golden brown and cooked through (no soft spots). Remove from oven and cool.

YIELDS 4 SERVINGS

GARDEN AND HERB SALAD
WITH GARLIC SHALLOT VINAIGRETTE

GARLIC SHALLOT VINAIGRETTE
2 tablespoons diced shallots
2 tablespoons minced garlic
1 tablespoon Dijon mustard
4 tablespoons champagne vinegar
4 tablespoons olive oil

GARDEN AND HERB SALAD
1 pound mixed greens, washed
1 tablespoon minced chives
2 tablespoons chervil leaves
2 tablespoons basil leaves, torn
2 tablespoons dill leaves
Salt

White pepper
½ cup grape tomatoes
½ cup yellow teardrop tomatoes
1 tablespoon olive oil
1 English cucumber, sliced lengthwise into 4 thin
   strips

Who can resist a fabulous, fresh green salad? An array of herbs and homemade vinaigrette give this recipe great flavor.

FOR THE GARLIC SHALLOT VINAIGRETTE:
In a mixing bowl, combine shallots, garlic, mustard and vinegar. Using a whisk, stir in olive oil.

FOR THE GARDEN AND HERB SALAD:
1.   In a large mixing bowl, combine greens, chives, chervil, basil and dill. Toss with Garlic Shallot Vinaigrette. Season to taste with salt and pepper.

2.   In a small mixing bowl, toss tomatoes and olive oil, and season to taste with salt and pepper.

3.   On each of four serving plates, create a ring with the cucumber strips and place greens inside of the ring. Place tomatoes around the salad.

YIELDS 4 SERVINGS

ASIAN BEEF SALAD
WITH SOUR SOY VINAIGRETTE

1 pound beef tenderloin, cut into 4 equal-size
   steaks
¼ cup Citrus Soy (see p. 22)
¼ cup peanut oil
1 pound Asian greens

16 slices lotus root
½ cup daikon, julienned

SOUR SOY VINAIGRETTE
¼ cup soy sauce
¼ cup rice wine vinegar

1 tablespoon ginger, minced
1 tablespoon garlic, minced
1 tablespoon scallion, minced
2 tablespoons grape seed oil

This is a classic Asian recipe that exhibits the Cypress flavor profiles of hot, sour, salty, sweet and bitter.

1. Place pieces of beef in a small container and cover with Citrus Soy.
2. Allow to marinate at least 2 hours.
3. Place a medium-size sauté pan over high heat. Add peanut oil.
4. Sear beef quickly on both sides, but long enough to allow for a good caramelized crust (approximately 1 1/2 minutes per side).
5. Place on paper towels to absorb oil.
6. Transfer to a cutting board and slice thinly.

7. In a large mixing bowl, combine Asian greens, lotus root and daikon with Sour Soy Vinaigrette. Incorporate evenly.
8. On four serving plates, place equal amounts of Asian greens. Lay sliced beef in front of greens and fan out the beef.

FOR THE SOY VINAIGRETTE:
In a small mixing bowl, combine all ingredients and incorporate evenly.

YIELDS 4 SERVINGS

CHEF DEIHL'S NOTES: *Following are some no-fail salad combinations based on seasonal harvests:*
Spring: beets, carrots, English peas, goat cheese
Summer: beans, cucumbers, herbs, figs, melon, summer squash, tomatoes, zucchini
Fall: apples, bleu cheese, mustard greens, nuts, Parmesan cheese, pears
Winter: dried fruits, duck, watercress, wilted greens

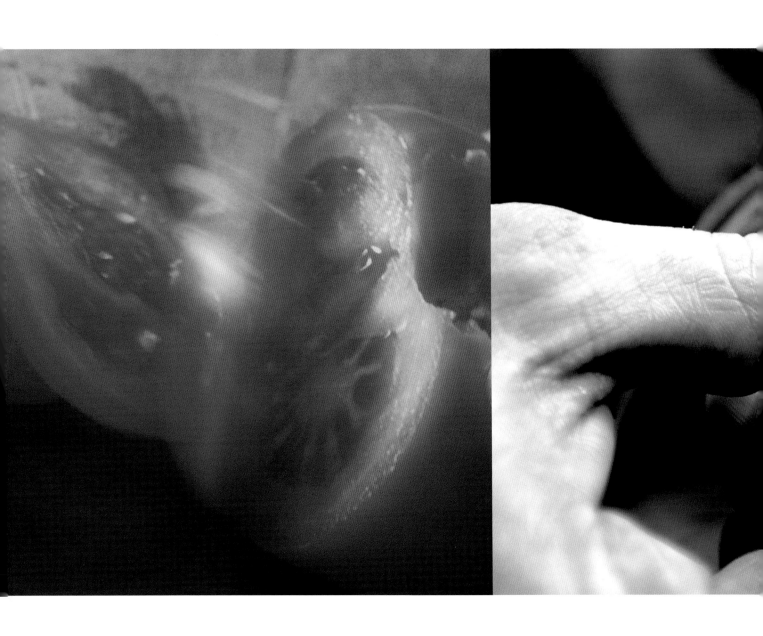

FROMAGE BLANC WITH DRIED FIG COMPOTE,
WATERCRESS AND AGED BALSAMIC

FROMAGE BLANC
10 cups milk
2 cups cream
¼ cup lemon juice
4 tablespoons salt

TOAST POINTS
2 loaves Honey Wheat Brioche (see p. 227)
¼ cup olive oil

DRIED FIG COMPOTE
½ cup dried figs, quartered
2 tablespoons honey

¼ cup brandy
1 teaspoon kosher salt
1 head living watercress, cut from roots and washed
Drizzle of olive oil
Salt and white pepper to taste
Aged Balsamic Vinegar
Finishing salt (Maldon)

Don't be daunted by the thought of homemade cheese. The first batch may be complicated, but the process gets easier with experience. The dried figs and balsamic vinegar give this cheese presentation a sweet flavor, making it perfect for the end of a meal.

FOR THE FROMAGE BLANC:
1. In a heavy saucepan, combine the milk and heavy cream. Place over low heat and bring to a boil, stirring occasionally so it does not stick to the bottom.
2. Add the lemon juice; stir until you see curds form in the liquid.
3. Remove from heat and strain through cheesecloth. The whey that comes through the cloth can be discarded.
4. When all the liquid is pressed out of the fromage, add the salt and incorporate evenly.
5. Wrap the cheese tightly in cheesecloth and press between two plates overnight.

FOR THE TOAST POINTS:
1. Preheat oven to 325 degrees.
2. Slice the brioche into 1/4-inch-thick slices. Place slices on a sheet pan greased with the olive oil.
3. Bake for 6 to 8 minutes, or until golden brown.

FOR THE DRIED FIG COMPOTE:
1. In a mixing bowl, combine all figs, honey, brandy and kosher salt and let stand overnight. The mixture should have a syrup-like consistency.
2. Directly before plating, toss the watercress with a drizzle of olive oil and season with salt and white pepper.
3. Cut the cheese into four pieces.
4. On each of four plates, place 1 toast point, then a piece of cheese on top of the toast point.
5. Place a spoonful of the fig compote on top of the cheese. Place another toast point on the side of the cheese, using the fig compote to hold it upright.
6. Place a few leaves of the watercress next to the cheese. Finish with a few drops of the vinegar and a sprinkle of the finishing salt.

PORTOBELLO MILLE-FEULLE
WITH BOURSIN CHEESE, SPINACH AND PORT WINE SYRUP

PORT WINE SYRUP
3 cups port wine

MILLE-FEULLE
5 sheets phyllo
¼ cup Clarified Butter (see p. 26)
2 tablespoons chopped thyme

2 tablespoons chopped basil
Salt
White pepper

PORTOBELLO MUSHROOMS
5 equal-size portobello mushrooms, stems
    removed
5 tablespoons olive oil

Salt
White pepper

TO ASSEMBLE
1½ cups Boursin cheese (see p. 175)
1 cup baby spinach
Maldon sea salt

This is a great cheese and crackers plate. Mille-feulle means a thousand leaves. In this preparation, the phyllo makes up the many layers. The Boursin cheese is made from scratch in the style of a true Boursin. If making the mille-feulle sounds too challenging, then make toast points from a baguette and use them.

FOR THE PORT WINE SYRUP:
1. Place the port wine in a small saucepan and bring to a simmer over medium heat.
2. Drop the temperature to low and reduce the port slowly by three-fourths; this will take about 1 1/2 hours. The port will become syrupy when finished.
3. Cool the port and place in a small squirt bottle.

FOR THE MILLE-FEULLE:
1. Preheat oven to 350 degrees.
2. Lay first phyllo sheet out lengthwise on a cutting board and brush lightly with the butter. Lay second sheet on top of first sheet of phyllo and brush with butter. Repeat this process with the remaining 3 sheets. Finish with the last bit of the butter and top with the chopped herbs and a light dusting of salt and pepper.
3. Using a ruler, cut the phyllo into two 3/4-x-6-inch pieces, producing 30 pieces. This can also be done by cutting the sheets in half lengthwise, then cutting into 3 equal pieces widthwise and then another 5 pieces lengthwise.
4. Place the pieces on a sheet tray and cover with another tray to keep the sheets flat.

5. Bake for 12 minutes and remove the top tray and bake for another 2 minutes. The mille-feulle should be crispy and golden brown.

FOR THE PORTOBELLO MUSHROOMS:
1. Place the mushrooms on a sheet pan with the tops facing up. Make sure the mushrooms are spread apart for even cooking. Rub the tops with a tablespoon of olive oil each. Season with salt and pepper.
2. Place in the oven and bake for 15 minutes. Mushrooms should flatten and release moisture. Remove and cool completely.
3. Slice each mushroom into 7 thin slices. Discard the end pieces.

FOR THE ASSEMBLY:
1. Place the cheese in a piping bag with a medium tip.
2. Squeeze an equal amount of cheese onto each piece of Mille-Feulle.
3. Place 4 leaves of baby spinach on top of cheese and finish with the sliced mushrooms. Drizzle with Port Wine Syrup and a sprinkle of Maldon sea salt.

YIELDS 4 SERVINGS

THAI SEAFOOD SALAD

4 ounces cream cheese
2 ounces fish sauce
2 tablespoons Thai Spice (see p. 185)
1 tablespoon cilantro leaves
1 tablespoon mint
½ tablespoon lemon grass (zested on a microplane)
1 teaspoon sambal oelek

2 gallons water
½ cup salt
½ pound squid (tubes sliced into rings)
½ pound squid tentacles, cleaned
½ pound large shrimp, peeled, deveined, split in half
½ pound lump crab

8 Thai basil leaves
8 mint leaves
8 cilantro leaves
1 tablespoon sliced chives
1 tablespoon Thai Spice (see p. 185)
Mint Oil (see p. 24)

A cream cheese base makes this the perfect summer salad; it's light, yet filling. The green curry paste is mild, giving the dish fragrance rather than heat.

1. Using a blender or food processor, combine cream cheese, fish sauce, 2 tablespoons Thai Spice, 1 tablespoon cilantro, 1 tablespoon mint, lemon grass and sambal. Purée until smooth.
2. Strain through a fine sieve with a rubber spatula.
3. Refrigerate overnight.
4. In a large pot, bring water and add salt to a boil.
5. In a large bowl, fill with ice and water. This will be used to shock the seafood after boiling.
6. Clean the squid, making sure there are no beaks or cartilage. Beaks are found in the center of the tentacles; remove with a paring knife. Cartilage is found in the tubes and can be removed by hand.

7. When salt water is boiling, add sliced squid and cook 45 seconds. Remove squid from water and shock in ice water. Add the squid tentacles to the boiling saltwater and boil for 45 seconds. Remove squid tentacles from water and shock in ice water. Add shrimp to the boiling saltwater and cook for 1 1/2 minutes. Remove and shock in ice water.
8. Remove ice cubes and strain water from seafood. Combine seafood with lump crab.
9. In a mixing bowl, combine seafood with cream cheese mixture.
10. Toss in herbs and incorporate evenly.
11. On four serving plates, place equal amounts of seafood salad. Garnish with a sprinkle of Thai Spice and a drizzle of Mint Oil.

YIELDS 4 SERVINGS

the recipes

Thai Coconut Chicken

Lobster Bisque with Butter-Poached Lobster and Chervil

Bacon and Oyster Stew

Asian Chicken Noodle Soup

Chilled Tomato Soup with Lump Crab and Basil Oil

Butternut Squash Soup with Duck Confit, Pecans, Fresh Nutmeg and
Maple Syrup

Chilled Pea Soup with Lobster and Mint Vinaigrette

The soups and stews at Cypress follow my mission to reflect a melting pot of flavors and world cuisines. Fresh, flavorful stocks are the keys to the successful preparation of these simple, elegant recipes which you will find useful in your growing kitchen repertoire.

From our classic Lobster Bisque and Oyster Stew to the cutting-edge Asian Chicken Noodle and Chilled Pea soups, the recipes here are versatile as dinner party starters or paired with a salad and bread for a light meal at home. As a departure from the traditional soup bowl, consider serving the puréed soups in espresso cups—or even shot glasses—for an *amuse bouche*. Once you have mastered the basics, get creative and keep in mind that a change in garnish can give a favorite soup a new personality.

THAI COCONUT CHICKEN

½ chicken (about 1½ pounds)
3 tablespoons canola oil
Salt
White pepper
2 tablespoons butter
1 cup baby shiitake mushrooms
½ cup julienned scallions
2 tablespoons mint leaves
2 tablespoons cilantro

2 teaspoons lime zest
2 tablespoons Thai Spice (see p. 185)
Mint Oil (see p. 24)

COCONUT CREAM
3 tablespoons chopped ginger
3 tablespoons chopped garlic
1 (12-ounce) can coconut milk
2 cups Chicken Stock (see p. 32)

¼ cup fish sauce
¼ cup mirin
¼ cup lime juice
2 kaffir lime leaves
3 tablespoons chopped cilantro
3 tablespoons chopped mint
3 tablespoons honey
1 small Thai green chili or 1 tablespoon sambal
   oelek

1. Preheat oven to 325 degrees.
2. In a roasting pan, place chicken skin side up. Rub chicken with oil, salt and pepper.
3. Roast chicken for 1 hour. Chicken should be caramelized well on the outside.
4. Remove from oven. Rest chicken for 10 minutes, or until cool enough to pull chicken apart with fingers. Latex gloves may help protect your fingers. Keep chicken warm.
5. Place sauté pan over medium heat. Add butter and shiitake mushrooms. Cook for 4 minutes until caramelized.
6. Combine mushrooms and chicken along with scallions, mint, cilantro and lime zest.
7. In four serving bowls, place 1 cup coconut cream. Divide chicken between the 4 bowls. Garnish with a sprinkle of Thai Spice and a drizzle of Mint Oil.

FOR THE COCONUT CREAM:

1. Combine all ingredients in a heavy-bottom saucepan and bring to a simmer over medium heat.
2. Cook for 20 minutes. Strain coconut broth into another saucepan and keep warm. Discard solids.

YIELDS 4 SERVINGS

LOBSTER BISQUE
WITH BUTTER-POACHED LOBSTER AND CHERVIL

¼ cup extra virgin olive oil

½ cup onion, large dice

¼ cup celery, large dice

¼ cup carrots, medium dice

1 head garlic, cut in half

2 (1¼-pound) lobsters, separated meat and shells
(see p. 79)

½ cup tomato paste

¼ cup brandy

1 cup white wine

4 cups water

¼ cup basil

2 tablespoons kosher salt

1 teaspoon white pepper

1 pinch cayenne pepper

¼ cup Roux (see right)

2 cups heavy cream

4 tablespoons cold butter

Beurre Fondue (see right)

12 chervil leaves

ROUX

¼ cup butter

¼ cup plus 3 tablespoons flour

BEURRE FONDUE

2 tablespoons water

1 pound cold butter (cut into cubes)

This is a Cypress original, requested many times over. We serve it with a Shrimp Cake garnish, but if you are cooking at home and need to use the remaining lobster meat, the recipe can easily transfer.

1. Place a stockpot over medium-high heat. Add olive oil, onion, celery, carrots and garlic and cook until vegetables start to break down, 5 to 6 minutes.

2. Add lobster shells and caramelize 4 to 5 minutes.

3. Add tomato paste and cook for another 5 to 6 minutes. Deglaze with brandy and white wine. Return to heat. Stir, scraping the bottom of the pan.

4. Add water, basil, salt and white pepper and cook for 25 minutes. Strain stock and discard lobster shells.

5. Place stock back on stove and bring to a simmer.

6. Using an immersion blender, add roux and purée until smooth. Cook for 5 minutes to cook out the starch.

7. Add heavy cream and butter and purée.

8. Strain through a fine sieve into a clean pot. Place over low heat and keep bisque hot.

9. Add lobster meat to Beurre Fondue and cook over low heat for 5 minutes.

10. In four soup bowls, place 1/2 a tail and 1 claw and meat from 1 knuckle, [1]. Garnish lobster with chervil leaves and finish with equal amounts of bisque. Serve immediately.

FOR THE ROUX:

1. Place a large saucepan over medium heat and add butter.

2. Melt butter completely and add flour.

3. Incorporate evenly and cook for 5 minutes.

FOR THE BEURRE FONDUE

1. Place a saucepan over medium heat. Add water and bring to a boil.

2. Slowly whisk in cold butter, adding butter one cube at a time. Lower temperature and continue to whisk until all butter has been incorporated. Mixture should be smooth and creamy.

3. Remove from heat and place in a warm location.

YIELDS 4 SERVINGS

BACON AND OYSTER STEW

1 pint shucked oysters (approximately 30 oysters)

¼ cup diced bacon

2 tablespoons minced garlic

2 tablespoons minced shallots

¼ cup all-purpose flour

½ cup sherry

2 cups Fish Fumet (see p. 35)

2 cups heavy cream

2 tablespoons Worcestershire sauce

2 teaspoons Tabasco

1 tablespoon lemon juice

½ tablespoon salt

Pinch of white pepper

1. Strain oysters, reserving the oyster liquor.

2. Place large saucepan over medium heat and add diced bacon. Render the bacon for 4 minutes. Bacon should be lightly caramelized.

3. Add garlic and shallots and sweat for 2 minutes, stirring constantly.

4. Add flour and stir until all fat is absorbed.

5. Add sherry, oyster liquor and Fish Fumet and bring to a low simmer.

6. Add heavy cream, Worcestershire sauce, Tabasco and lemon juice. Continue to simmer for 5 minutes.

7. Add salt, pepper and oysters. Cook just until oysters plump.

8. In four serving bowls, ladle equal amounts of oysters and oyster broth.

YIELDS 4 SERVINGS

ASIAN CHICKEN NOODLE SOUP

2 gallons water

¼ cup salt

8 ounces dried udon noodles

2 tablespoons diced ginger

2 tablespoons diced shallots

2 tablespoons diced garlic

½ cup mirin

3 cups Chicken Stock (see p. 32)

½ cup mushroom soy

2 chicken breasts, sliced thin

8 ounces baby shiitake mushrooms

4 ounces mizuna

16 cilantro leaves

A good-for-you soup that's comfort food from another continent. The large, wheaty Japanese udon noodles remind me of mom's dumplings.

1. In a large pot, combine water and salt. Bring to a boil and add dried udon noodles. Reduce to a simmer and cook for 12 minutes. Check noodles to make sure they are tender. Strain and rinse with water. The noodles can be stored covered in water until ready to use.

2. In a large pot, add ginger, shallots, garlic and mirin. Bring to a quick boil; this will cook the alcohol out of the mirin.

3. Add stock and mushroom soy and bring to a simmer. Add the sliced chicken, shiitake mushrooms and poach for 2 to 3 minutes.

4. In four serving bowls, combine equal amounts of noodles, mizuna and cilantro leaves. Pour equal amounts of chicken, mushrooms and broth over the noodles and serve immediately.

YIELDS 4 SERVINGS

CHILLED TOMATO SOUP WITH LUMP CRAB AND BASIL OIL

SOUP
2 cups plum tomatoes, blanched, peeled, seeded
    and diced
¼ cup champagne vinegar
1 tablespoon salt
¼ teaspoon white pepper

2 tablespoons sugar
1 teaspoon lemon zest

LUMP CRABMEAT
½ pound lump crabmeat
2 ounces cream cheese, room temperature

1 tablespoon minced chives
½ teaspoon salt
Pinch of white pepper
1 cup yellow teardrop tomatoes
Basil Oil (see p. 24)

This simple recipe is best made during peak tomato season, which falls in the lowcountry during mid to late summer. It's outstanding on its own, but different garnishes can change the personality of the soup.

FOR THE SOUP:
1. Place all ingredients in a blender and purée until smooth.
2. Strain tomato purée through a chinois. Refrigerate and keep cold.

FOR THE LUMP CRABMEAT:
1. In a small mixing bowl, combine crabmeat, cream cheese, chives, salt and pepper.
2. Using a 3-inch ring mold in the center of four serving bowls, place crabmeat inside each ring mold and pack tightly. Pack equal amounts of tomatoes on top of crabmeat.
3. Pour equal amounts of tomato soup around each ring mold.
4. Remove ring mold. Garnish with Basil Oil.

YIELDS 4 SERVINGS

BUTTERNUT SQUASH SOUP
WITH DUCK CONFIT, PECANS, FRESH NUTMEG AND MAPLE SYRUP

2 tablespoons butter

1 tablespoon minced garlic

1 tablespoon minced shallots

3 cups butternut squash, peeled, seeded and cubed

½ cup white wine

3 cups water

1 bouquet garni (sage and thyme)

½ tablespoon nutmeg (grated on microplane)

1 tablespoon salt

1 teaspoon white pepper

8 tablespoons cold butter

Duck Confit (using 2 legs) (see p. 65)

½ cup pecans

2 tablespoons butter

2 tablespoons maple syrup

1 whole nutmeg

Chive Oil (see p. 24)

This is a purist's soup, as all of the ingredients work together to bring out the flavor of the squash. There is no cream in this recipe, but the Duck Confit adds a little fat flavor. At Cypress, we use a Bourbon Maple Syrup from Mikuna Wild Harvest in Tennessee.

1. Place a large pot over medium heat. Add butter, garlic and shallots. Sweat until translucent; keep the mixture moving.

2. Add butternut squash and white wine. Cook until wine has almost evaporated, 7 to 8 minutes.

3. Add water and bouquet garni, bring to a simmer for 20 minutes. Squash should be soft.

4. Add nutmeg, salt and pepper. Using an immersion blender, purée until smooth.

5. Add cold butter and incorporate. Strain soup and keep hot.

6. Pull meat off duck legs. Discard fat and bones.

7. Place sauté pan over medium heat. Add butter and pecans to pan. Toast for 2 minutes. Lower temperature to low.

8. Add pulled duck and maple syrup and heat through.

9. In four bowls, place equal amounts of butternut squash soup. Spoon equal amounts of pecans and duck meat in the center of the soup. Using microplane, grate nutmeg over dishes. Garnish with Chive Oil and serve immediately.

YIELDS 4 SERVINGS

CHILLED PEA SOUP WITH LOBSTER
AND MINT VINAIGRETTE

4 cups blanched English peas
2½ cups water
2 tablespoons salt
1½ teaspoons white pepper
1 (1¼-pound) lobster (see p. 79)
¼ cup blanched English peas

2 ounces pea tendrils
Mint Oil (see p. 24)

MINT VINAIGRETTE
3 tablespoons champagne vinegar
3 tablespoons extra virgin olive oil

½ tablespoon minced shallot
½ tablespoon minced garlic
1 tablespoon finely chopped mint
1 teaspoon salt
1 teaspoon pink peppercorns, crushed

This is a lovely composed soup with distinctive textures—puréed peas, orzo pasta and lobster—for added interest. The bright green color makes it a perfect starter for spring and summer meals.

1. Place English peas in a food processor. Purée until smooth.
2. Press peas through a tamis. Discard any pea mixture that will not go through the tamis.
3. Place the pea purée and water in a blender. Purée until smooth. Season with salt and pepper.
4. Strain pea purée through a chinois. Refrigerate and keep cold.
5. Split lobster in half. Remove tail meat and slice into pieces. Place lobster into a small mixing bowl.
6. Remove meat from claw and knuckles. Mix meat with tail meat.
7. Toss the lobster meat with the English peas and Mint Vinaigrette.
8. In four serving bowls place equal amounts of the pea soup. Place the lobster and peas in the center of the bowl and garnish with the pea tendrils and a drizzle of Mint Oil.

FOR THE MINT VINAIGRETTE:
1. Combine all ingredients in mint vinaigrette and incorporate evenly.

YIELDS 4 SERVINGS

{ F I S H   A N D   5   S H E L L F I S H }

the recipes

Smoked Salmon Wellington with Gruyère Potato Fondue, Asparagus and Lemon Beurre Blanc

Grilled Wahoo with Sweet Corn Fricassee, Rock Shrimp and Lacy Potatoes

Crisp Wasabi Tuna with Edamame, Baby Shiitake Mushrooms and Chili Garlic Glaze

Braised Wreckfish with Eggplant, Baby Squash, Tomatoes and Crispy Squash Blossom

Serrano Wrapped Mahi-mahi with Truffle Grits, Asparagus, Grape Tomatoes and Sautéed Shrimp

Seafood Pot with Baby Fennel, Tomatoes and Shellfish Broth

Seared Golden Tilefish with Edamame, Baby Shiitake Mushrooms and Thai Coconut Cream

Shrimp and Sausage with Grape Tomatoes, Mint and Garlic Broth and Goat Cheese Grits

Palmetto Bass en Papillote with Summer Beans and Tomatoes

Grilled Swordfish with Confit Potatoes, Artichokes and Lemon Butter

Szechwan Pepper Crusted Tuna with Jerusalem Artichokes, Mizuna, Braised Belgian Endive, Capers and Feta

Here in the South Carolina Lowcountry, we are blessed with a bounty of seafood, from the fish and shellfish that live in our temperate rivers to those that swim in deeper waters off the coast. The menu at Cypress has some fantastic seafood entrées and we run specials throughout the year based on harvest seasons and seafood populations.

During my time at Cypress, I have been very involved with the South Carolina Aquarium's Sustainable Seafood Initiative. The project's goal is to educate the public on wise seafood choices and the consumption of environmentally friendly, locally captured seafood. It's imperative that restaurant chefs and the dining community make smart choices if we want to continue to have strong fish populations in the United States and around the world. I hope that home cooks will share our concern.

In the pages that follow, you will find some familiar preparations rendered "Cypress-style." For example, the unexpected Salmon Wellington and the Shrimp and Sausage that surprises with lamb sausage and goat cheese.

SMOKED SALMON WELLINGTON
WITH GRUYÈRE POTATO FONDUE, ASPARAGUS AND LEMON BEURRE BLANC

DUXELLES

3 tablespoons butter

2 tablespoons minced shallots

1 tablespoon minced garlic

¼ cup chopped crimini mushrooms

¼ cup chopped portobello mushrooms, stems
   removed

¼ cup chopped shiitake mushrooms, stems removed

¼ cup red wine

2 tablespoons foie gras

1 tablespoon thyme

1 tablespoon basil

GRUYÈRE POTATO FONDUE

3 pounds Yukon gold potatoes, peeled and cut
   into ½-inch-thick rounds

2 tablespoons salt

1½ cups heavy cream

½ cup grated gruyère cheese

½ cup butter, cut into cubes

1½ tablespoons salt

1½ teaspoons white pepper

LEMON BEURRE BLANC

½ cup white wine

2 tablespoons lemon juice

1 tablespoon shallot, chopped

4 sprigs thyme

4 black peppercorns

½ pound cold butter, cut into cubes

Salt

One of Cypress's signature entrées, Smoked Salmon Wellington is our spin on the classic Wellington preparation. It's an incredibly rich dish that's a great entrée for special occasion entertaining.

This is a time intensive recipe, but several elements, including the Duxelles and the Smoked Salmon, may be done a day in advance. If you don't want to bother with smoking the fish, you can still make this dish with regular salmon fillets. Also, don't overcook the salmon; it is best when served at a medium temperature.

FOR THE DUXELLES:

1. Place a large sauté pan over medium-high heat. Add butter, shallots and garlic. Cook for 3 minutes until caramelized.

2. Add mushrooms and continue to sauté for 5 minutes. Add red wine and cook 3 to 4 minutes, or until most of the moisture is cooked out.

3. Add foie gras, thyme and basil. Incorporate evenly.

4. Transfer mixture to a food processor and purée until mixture is even.

5. Cool mixture completely and set aside or refrigerate for later use.

FOR THE GRUYÈRE POTATO FONDUE:

1. In a large pot, add potatoes and salt and cover with water.

2. Place over medium heat and cook for 25 minutes. Potatoes should split when pierced with a fork.

3. Transfer the potatoes to a colander and drain.

4. Place a food mill with the smallest screen over the pot you cooked the potatoes in. Work the hot potatoes through the food mill.

5. Add the heavy cream and gruyère cheese to the potatoes and fold in evenly. The cheese will get stringy as it melts.

6. Stir in the butter cubes until melted. The potatoes should have a velvety consistency.

7. Season with the salt and pepper and incorporate evenly. Adjust seasoning if needed.

8. Keep the potatoes in a warm area. If you have a lid, use it or wrap tightly with food film.

FOR THE LEMON BEURRE BLANC:

1. In a saucepan, combine the white wine, lemon juice, shallot, thyme and peppercorns. Place over medium-low heat.

2. Reduce to about 3 tablespoons. Reduce the temperature if it is boiling rapidly; you only want a low simmer.

3. When reduced, slowly whisk in the cold butter, one cube at a time. Mixture should be smooth and creamy. Season with salt to taste.

4. Strain through a fine sieve and keep warm.

Continued on next page

ASPARAGUS WITH SHALLOTS AND GARLIC

2 tablespoons butter

2 tablespoons thinly sliced shallots

1 teaspoon minced garlic

1 cup asparagus spears, blanched and cut into
   1-inch pieces

Salt

White pepper

SMOKED SALMON WELLINGTON

(Salmon can be smoked a day in advance)

4 (6-ounce) pieces salmon, skin removed

Salt

White pepper

5 sheets phyllo

¼ cup Clarified Butter (see p. 26)

¼ cup olive oil

FOR THE ASPARAGUS WITH SHALLOTS AND GARLIC:

1. Place a sauté pan over medium heat and add the butter. When butter starts to melt, add the shallots and garlic. Sweat until translucent.

2. Add the asparagus pieces and cook for 2 minutes. Asparagus should be hot through. Taste to check. Season with salt and pepper.

3. Keep warm by covering with a lid or wrapping with food film.

FOR THE SMOKED SALMON WELLINGTON:

1. Season the salmon with salt and pepper.

2. If you are going to smoke the salmon, start with the next step; if not, proceed to step 6.

3. Heat a small amount of wood chips in your grill until smoldering. Close the lid to trap the smoke. Try not to create heat with the grill, as this will cook your salmon.

4. Working fast, place the salmon in the now smoking grill and cover with the lid. Let the salmon sit for 15 minutes to absorb the smoke flavor.

5. Remove the salmon from the grill, place on a plate, wrap tightly with food film and place in refrigerator. (Wrapping tightly will trap the smoke flavor in the fish.)

6. Lay first phyllo sheet out lengthwise on a flat work surface and brush lightly with the butter. Lay second sheet on top of first sheet of phyllo and brush with butter. Repeat this process with the remaining 3 sheets.

7. Add the Duxelles to the bottom half of the phyllo sheets. Make sure that the paste is even thickness.

8. Place the smoked salmon pieces on top of the Duxelles. Cut the phyllo the same width as the salmon pieces.

9. Roll the salmon pieces, Duxelles and phyllo up. Make sure the Duxelles only cover the salmon on the first revolution. (You don't want it to look like a jellyroll.)

10. Place a large sauté pan over medium-high heat and add the olive oil.

11. Add the wrapped salmon pieces to the pan and sear for 1 minute. Flip the salmon and sear on remaining sides for the same length of time. This will ensure that the fish is cooked evenly.

12. Remove from the pan and place on paper towels to absorb excess oil.

13. Transfer salmon to a cutting board and slice each piece into three pieces.

14. On four serving plates, place equal amounts of potatoes in the center. Using a kitchen spoon, press down on the potatoes and drag the spoon. This will create a well where you will place equal amounts of asparagus. Place 3 salmon pieces on top of the asparagus. Place the sauce around the plate and serve immediately.

YIELDS 4 SERVINGS

GRILLED WAHOO WITH SWEET CORN FRICASSEE,
ROCK SHRIMP AND LACY POTATOES

CORN PURÉE

2 tablespoons butter

1½ cups corn kernels

¼ cup minced celery

¼ cup minced onion

1½ cups Corn Stock (see p. 32)

2 teaspoons salt

1 teaspoon white pepper

2 tablespoons butter

SWEET CORN FRICASSEE

2 tablespoons butter

¼ cup minced onion

¼ cup minced celery

2 cups yellow corn kernels

½ pound rock shrimp, peeled

1 tablespoon chopped basil

Salt

White pepper

LACY POTATOES

1 gallon peanut oil or canola oil

2 large russet potatoes

Fine sea salt

WAHOO

4 (6-ounce) portions wahoo

Salt

White pepper

Wahoo is the fastest fish in the ocean, hence it's lean and can be dry if overcooked. I suggest cooking the fish until it's halfway done and removing it from the heat to rest for a perfectly moist finale. The lacy potatoes are a crispy foil to the wahoo and corn fricassee.

FOR THE CORN PURÉE:

1. Place a medium-size saucepan over medium heat. Add 2 tablespoons butter, corn, celery and onion. Sauté until translucent.

2. Add stock, salt and pepper and cook for 5 minutes. If liquid starts to boil, lower heat.

3. Remove mixture from heat and purée with an immersion blender. Add the last 2 tablespoons of butter and purée until smooth.

4. Strain corn purée and keep warm.

FOR THE SWEET CORN FRICASSEE:

1. Place sauté pan over medium heat and add butter, onion, and celery. Sweat until onions and celery are translucent.

2. Add corn and shrimp and cook 4 minutes. Add basil and season to taste with salt and pepper.

3. Remove from heat and keep warm.

FOR THE LACY POTATOES:

1. Place oil in large saucepan. Attach a thermometer to the side of the pan and heat oil to 350 degrees.

2. Using a Japanese mandolin setup with wide teeth and medium thickness, slice the potatoes into a bowl.

3. Cover the potatoes with water to remove excess starch. Pull the potatoes out of the water and drain in a colander. Place on paper towels and pat dry.

4. Fry the potatoes in small batches for 2 minutes. They should be crispy and golden brown when done. Place on paper towels to absorb excess grease.

5. Season with fine sea salt.

FOR THE WAHOO:

1. Season wahoo with salt and pepper.

2. Grill wahoo 2 to 3 minutes on each side. Wahoo will be dry if overcooked.

3. In four serving bowls, ladle equal amounts of corn purée. Place equal amounts of shrimp and corn fricassee on top of the purée. Place grilled wahoo on top of Sweet Corn Fricassee, garnish with Lacy Potatoes and serve.

YIELDS 4 SERVINGS

CRISP WASABI TUNA
WITH EDAMAME, BABY SHIITAKE MUSHROOMS AND CHILI GARLIC GLAZE

5 sheets phyllo
¼ cup Clarified Butter (see p. 26)
4 tablespoons wasabi powder
¼ cup pineapple juice
4 (6-ounce) pieces sashimi tuna, cut into rectangles
¼ cup peanut oil or canola oil

CHILI GARLIC GLAZE
¼ cup rice wine vinegar
½ cup sugar

1 tablespoon fine sea salt
1 tablespoon minced garlic
1 tablespoon minced ginger
½ tablespoon sambal oelek
½ tablespoon chopped cilantro
½ tablespoon chopped mint
½ tablespoon chopped basil

EDAMAME AND BABY SHIITAKE MUSHROOMS
2 tablespoons peanut oil
¾ cup baby shiitake mushrooms
¾ cup edamame (green soybeans)
¼ Chili Soy (see p. 22)
1 tablespoon honey
1 teaspoon sambal oelek
2 tablespoons cold butter
Salt and freshly ground white pepper

This dish is the most requested item on the Cypress menu. It's incredibly flavorful and hits tastes buds with just the right notes of hot, sour, salty and sweet. When shopping for the fish, ask your fishmonger to cut the tuna in long, block-shaped pieces to help with the assembly for cooking.

1. Lay first phyllo sheet out lengthwise on a flat work surface and brush lightly with the butter. Lay second sheet on top of first sheet of phyllo and brush with butter. Repeat this process with the remaining 3 sheets.
2. In a mixing bowl, combine wasabi powder and pineapple juice and incorporate to make a smooth paste.
3. Add the wasabi paste to the bottom half of the phyllo sheets. Make sure that the paste is an even thickness.
4. Place the blocks of tuna on top of the wasabi paste. Cut the phyllo the same width as the tuna pieces.
5. Roll the tuna, wasabi, and phyllo up. Make sure the wasabi only covers the tuna on the first revolution. (You don't want it to look like a jellyroll.)
6. Place a large sauté pan over medium-high heat. Add oil.
7. Add the wrapped tuna pieces to the sauté pan and sear for 1 minute on each side. All sides should be golden brown and should appear to be cooked the same when looking at the ends of the pieces.

8. Transfer to a cutting board and slice each piece in thirds.
9. On four serving plates, place equal amounts of edamame and baby shiitake mushrooms. Place 3 slices of tuna on top. Finish with 2 tablespoons of Chili Garlic Glaze per plate.

FOR THE CHILI GARLIC GLAZE:

1. In a saucepan, combine rice wine vinegar, sugar and salt. Place over medium-high heat and reduce by one-fourth. Mixture should have a syrup-like consistency.
2. Remove from heat and add garlic, ginger and sambal. Incorporate evenly and allow mixture to cool completely.
3. Add cilantro, mint and basil to cooled mixture. Adding herbs to mixture when hot will cause herbs to turn brown.
4. Place in a container and keep refrigerated.

FOR THE EDAMAME AND BABY SHIITAKE:

1. Heat the oil in a saucepan over high heat. Sauté the shiitake mushrooms for about 2 to 3 minutes.
2. Reduce the heat to medium and add the edamame and Chili Soy. Sauté for another minute; the Chili Soy should be syrupy.
3. Remove from heat and finish by slowly stirring in the butter. Season to taste with salt and pepper.

YIELDS 4 SERVINGS

BRAISED WRECKFISH WITH EGGPLANT,
BABY SQUASH, TOMATOES AND CRISPY SQUASH BLOSSOM

EGGPLANT, BABY SQUASH AND TOMATOES

1 gallon canola oil

2 cups water

3 tablespoons salt

½ cup baby Japanese eggplant, sliced into coins

3 tablespoons olive oil

½ cup baby zucchini, sliced into coins

½ cup baby squash, sliced into coins

3 tablespoons water

4 tablespoons Squash Blossom Butter (see p. 25)

½ cup grape tomatoes

1 tablespoon chopped basil

Salt

White pepper

1 gallon canola oil

TEMPURA-FRIED SQUASH BLOSSOM

1 cup cornstarch

1 cup all-purpose flour

1½ cups cold soda water

4 squash blossoms, with stem

Fine sea salt

BRAISED WRECKFISH

4 (6-ounce) fillets wreckfish

Salt

White pepper

3 tablespoons olive oil

3 cups Fish Fumet (see p. 35)

4 tablespoons Soffrito (see p. 27)

1 tablespoon chopped basil

The tempura-fried squash blossom is an elegant edible garnish for this lovely fish entrée. Soaking the eggplant in salted water prior to frying cuts the bitterness of the end product.

FOR THE EGGPLANT, BABY SQUASH AND TOMATOES:

1. In a large pot, heat canola oil to 300 degrees.
2. As the oil heats, soak the eggplant in the two cups of salted water for 10 minutes, drain and pat dry before frying.
3. Add eggplant to hot canola oil and cook for 4 minutes, stirring frequently.
4. Remove eggplant from oil and place on paper towels to absorb excess oil.
5. Place a large sauté pan over medium heat and add olive oil, zucchini, squash, and the fried eggplant. Cook for 3 minutes. Zucchini and squash should be soft on the outside, but still have a firm center.
6. Lower the heat and add 3 tablespoons water and Squash Blossom Butter, 1 tablespoon at a time. The butter will emulsify with the water and appear creamy.
7. Remove from heat. Stir in grape tomatoes and basil and season with salt and pepper to taste.

FOR THE TEMPURA-FRIED SQUASH BLOSSOM:

1. Reheat canola oil to 350 degrees.
2. In a medium-size mixing bowl, combine cornstarch, flour and cold soda water. Whip until incorporated. Keep cold until ready to use.
3. Holding squash blossoms by the stem, dip only the flowers into the tempura batter. Remove from batter and add to hot oil. Fry for 4 minutes. Flowers should be crispy and translucent.
4. Place on paper towels to absorb excess grease. Season with fine sea salt. Keep warm.

FOR THE BRAISED WRECKFISH:

1. Preheat oven to 350 degrees.
2. Season wreckfish with salt and pepper.
3. Place a large saucepan over medium-high heat and add olive oil and wreckfish to pan. Sear for 3 minutes on one side. Remove fish from pan and place on paper towels. Drain excess oil from pan and add Fish Fumet, Soffrito and basil to pan.
4. Place wreckfish, seared side up, in pan with fumet and transfer to oven.
5. Braise fish for 6 minutes. Fish should give slightly when pressed with finger.
6. On four serving plates, place an equal amount of the vegetables and top with the braised wreckfish. Top the wreckfish with a Fried Squash Blossom.

YIELDS 4 SERVINGS

SERRANO WRAPPED MAHI-MAHI
WITH TRUFFLE GRITS, ASPARAGUS, GRAPE TOMATOES AND SAUTÉED SHRIMP

TRUFFLE GRITS CAKE

3 cups water

¾ cup stone-ground white grits

3 tablespoons butter

¼ cup heavy cream

4 tablespoons Truffle Butter (see p. 26)

4 tablespoons cornmeal

¼ cup canola oil

SERRANO WRAPPED MAHI-MAHI AND SHRIMP

5 (5-ounce) mahi-mahi fillets, skin removed, blood line removed

4 paper-thin slices of Serrano ham (can substitute prosciutto)

2 ounces olive oil

6 large local white shrimp (peeled and deveined)

3 ounces white wine

4 tablespoons cold butter

Juice from 1 lemon

½ cup grape tomatoes, sliced in half

3 tablespoons chopped basil

1 teaspoon salt

Pinch white pepper

1 cup asparagus tips

Mahi-mahi (commonly known as dolphin) is one of the most sustainable fish swimming in our oceans. The thinly sliced Serrano ham offers just enough salt to flavor the fish, while local shrimp (I prefer the 21/25 per pound count) make for a delicious sauce. A rich truffle grits cake provides a dense, crispy pedestal for the final presentation.

FOR THE TRUFFLE GRITS CAKE:

1. Bring water to a boil. Add grits and cook 5 minutes over medium-low heat, stirring constantly until the water is absorbed and the grits are slightly creamy.

2. Remove from heat, put a lid on the pot and let sit for 40 minutes.

3. Add remaining ingredients and stir until the butter is completely melted.

4. Pour the grits into a greased 8 x 8 inch baking pan. Place in refrigerator and allow to set 3 hours.

5. When the grits have become firm, remove from pan and place on a cutting board.

6. Using a 3-inch ring mold, cut the grits into four circles.

7. Dust the grits with the cornmeal.

8. Place a large sauté pan over medium-high heat. Add canola oil and grits cakes. Sear 2 minutes on each side.

9. Remove from pan and keep warm.

FOR THE SERRANO WRAPPED MAHI-MAHI AND SHRIMP:

1. Wrap each piece of mahi-mahi in the Serrano ham.

2. Place a sauté pan over medium-high heat and add olive oil.

3. Add the mahi-mahi to the pan. Sear on first side 2 minutes, flip, and add shrimp.

4. Continue to cook 2 to 3 minutes. Remove mahi-mahi and shrimp from the pan. Deglaze pan with white wine and reduce liquid by half, 2 minutes.

5. Over low heat, stir in the cold butter until melted and creamy. Add lemon juice, tomatoes, basil and salt and pepper.

6. Place a sauté pan over medium heat and add the asparagus to the pan and cook 1 to 2 minutes.

7. On four serving plates, place a grits cake and top with asparagus and mahi-mahi. Place equal amounts of the tomato mixture on top of the fish. Finally, spoon the sauce and shrimp around the fish.

YIELDS 4 SERVINGS

SEEFOOD POT
WITH BABY FENNEL, TOMATOES AND SHELLFISH BROTH

2 tablespoons olive oil

4 cloves garlic, peeled

8 heads baby fennel, cut in half (tops removed and washed well)

½ cup white wine

1 preserved lemon, chopped, plus 1 tablespoon juice

2 cups water

1 pound monkfish, boneless fillets (each cut into 2 inch pieces)

Salt

White pepper

2 tablespoons olive oil

½ cup red onion, thinly sliced

¼ cup Soffrito (see p. 27)

1 cup Shellfish Stock (see p. 35)

12 little neck clams, purged and well scrubbed

½ pound mussels, well scrubbed

12 large shrimp, peeled and deveined

1 cup grape tomatoes, halved

½ tablespoon chopped basil

1 tablespoon chervil leaves

A lot of love goes into this intensely flavored, slow cooking seafood dish.

1.   Place a small saucepan over medium heat. Add the oil, garlic cloves and baby fennel. Sweat for 3 minutes. Add the white wine and chopped preserved lemon and cook for another 3 minutes; the wine should be reduced by half. Drop the temperature to medium-low, add the water and cook for 30 minutes. The baby fennel should be soft when pierced with a knife. Remove pan from heat and cool.

2.   Remove the fennel and the garlic cloves from the pan and place in a bowl. Strain lemon broth over the fennel and garlic. Store in the liquid until ready to use.

3.   Season the monkfish pieces with salt and pepper.

4.   Place a large pot over medium-high heat. Add the olive oil,

onion and Soffrito and lightly caramelize for 3 minutes.

5.   Add the stock, baby fennel, garlic and lemon broth to the pot and bring to a simmer. Add the monkfish pieces and cook 2 minutes.

6.   Reduce heat to medium to keep the pot at a simmer.

7.   Add the clams to the pot. Cook for 1 minute, then add the mussels. Stir the pot to cook the seafood evenly. Add the shrimp and cook 3 minutes. The monkfish and shrimp should be cooked at the same time the clams and mussels start to open.

8.   Remove the pot from heat. Strain the seafood from the broth into another pan and stir in the tomatoes and basil. Place broth back on the heat.

9.   In four serving bowls, place equal amounts of the mixed seafood. Pour the broth over the seafood and garnish with the chervil leaves.

YIELDS 4 SERVINGS

SEARED GOLDEN TILEFISH
WITH EDAMAME, BABY SHIITAKE MUSHROOMS AND THAI COCONUT CREAM

THAI COCONUT CREAM

3 tablespoons chopped fresh ginger

3 tablespoons chopped fresh garlic

1 (12-ounce) can coconut milk

¼ cup fish sauce

¼ cup mirin

3 tablespoons rice wine vinegar

2 kaffir lime leaves

¼ cup fresh lime juice

3 tablespoons chopped cilantro

2 tablespoons chopped mint

3 tablespoons honey

1 small Thai chile or 2 teaspoons sambal oelek

EDAMAME AND BABY SHIITAKE MUSHROOMS

2 tablespoons peanut oil

¾ cup baby shiitake mushrooms

¾ cup edamame (green soybeans)

¼ Chili Soy (see p. 22)

2 tablespoons cold butter

Salt and freshly ground white pepper

GOLDEN TILEFISH

1½ pounds golden tilefish fillets, cut into 4 equal-size portions

Salt and freshly ground white pepper

¼ cup peanut oil

2 tablespoons butter

Mint Oil (see p. 24)

Scallion curls

Golden tilefish is one of the most beautiful in the sea, producing a light flaky texture when cooked. I choose to sear the smaller fish to preserve the moisture. Tilefish is in season along the South Carolina coast from May to July. It can be substituted with wreckfish, grouper, or salmon, depending upon seasonality and freshness. The coconut cream can be made as far as two days in advance.

FOR THE THAI COCONUT CREAM:

1. Combine all ingredients in a heavy-bottom saucepot and bring to a simmer over medium heat. Cook for 20 to 25 minutes.
2. Season to taste, strain and keep warm.

FOR THE EDAMAME AND BABY SHIITAKE MUSHROOMS:

1. Heat the oil in a saucepan over high heat. Sauté the shiitake mushrooms for about 2 to 3 minutes.
2. Reduce the heat to medium and add the edamame and Chili Soy. Sauté for another minute; the Chili Soy should be syrupy. Remove from heat and finish by slowly stirring the butter in. Season to taste with salt and pepper.

FOR THE GOLDEN TILEFISH:

1. Using paper towels, dry the surface of the fish. Season the fillets with a dusting of salt and white pepper.
2. Place a large sauté pan over high heat and add the oil.
3. Add the golden tile to the pan and sear the fillets until golden brown, about 2 minutes. Flip the fillets over, lower the temperature to medium-high, add the butter and cook for another 2 minutes.
4. Remove the fish from pan and place on paper towels and pat dry.
5. In four dinner bowls, place two spoonfuls of edamame and shiitake mushrooms.
6. Place the fish on top of the edamame and mushrooms.
7. Ladle Thai Coconut Cream around the fish. Garnish with Mint Oil and scallion curls.

YIELDS 4 SERVINGS

SHRIMP AND SAUSAGE
WITH GRAPE TOMATOES, MINT AND GARLIC BROTH AND GOAT CHEESE GRITS

LAMB SAUSAGE
1 pound lamb, cubed
2 tablespoons chopped shallots
2 tablespoons crushed garlic
1 tablespoon rosemary
1½ tablespoons salt
2 teaspoons white pepper
4 tablespoons extra virgin olive oil
½ pound caul fat

TO ASSEMBLE
Goat Cheese Grits (see p. 209)
2 tablespoons olive oil
1 cup leeks, washed, halved, thinly sliced
1 pound large shrimp, peeled and deveined
  (save shells to make stock)
1½ cups Shellfish Stock (see p. 35)
½ cup yellow teardrop tomatoes, cut in half
½ cup grape tomatoes, cut in half

Salt
White pepper
1 tablespoon chopped mint
2 tablespoons cold butter
Mint Oil (see p. 24)

This recipe is my take on the classic lowcountry meal of Shrimp and Grits. The Lamb Sausage is a natural with the mint broth and the Goat Cheese Grits. If you are not up to making your own sausage, it's usually available at higher end grocers.

FOR THE LAMB SAUSAGE:
1. In a mixing bowl, combine the lamb, shallots, garlic, rosemary, salt, pepper and olive oil, **[1]**. Mix evenly, cover and refrigerate overnight.
2. Preheat oven to 350 degrees.
3. Using a meat grinder attached with the medium blade and set on a slow speed, grind the mixture, **[2]**. Fold the ground meat together, incorporating lightly.
4. Divide the ground meat into eight equal size balls, form into small logs and prepare to wrap the sausage.

5. Place the caul fat, **[3]**, out on a cutting board. Place the sausage on top of the caul fat and roll around sausage, **[4]**. Tightly fold in the ends and cut the caul fat. Repeat for the remaining amount of sausage.
6. Place the rolled sausage on a sheet pan and bake for 20 minutes.
7. Allow sausage to cool completely before cutting; the fat and juices will run out if cut while it is still hot.
8. When the sausage is cool, slice on a bias. Keep refrigerated until ready to use.

FOR ASSEMBLY:
1. Prepare Goat Cheese Grits and keep warm.
2. Place a large sauté pan over medium-high heat and add the oil. When the oil is hot, add the leeks and sauté for 2 minutes. The leeks should sweat quickly and not brown. If they start to brown, drop the temperature.
3. Add the shrimp and cook for 2 minutes. Increase the temperature to high and add the stock; reduce by half for 3 minutes. Remove from heat and mix in the tomatoes. Season to taste with salt and pepper, add the chopped mint and incorporate the butter.
4. In four serving bowls, place equal amounts of grits. Place equal amounts of Lamb Sausage on top. Spoon equal amounts of shrimp, tomatoes, leeks and broth on top of the grits. Garnish with Mint Oil.

YIELDS 4 SERVINGS

PALMETTO BASS EN PAPILLOTE
WITH SUMMER BEANS AND TOMATOES

4 (1-pound) hybrid bass (head and backbone removed and scaled)
4 tablespoons extra virgin olive oil
1 tablespoon lemon zest
1 tablespoon Maldon sea salt
1½ teaspoons white pepper

1 tablespoon chopped thyme leaves
2 tablespoons butter
½ cup haricots verts, blanched and cut into small rounds
½ cup edamame
¼ cup yellow teardrop tomatoes, cut in half

¼ cup grape tomatoes, cut in half
2 tablespoon chives, minced
1 tablespoon Lemon Butter (see p. 25)
Salt
White pepper
Maldon sea salt

Palmetto bass is a mild sweet fish prized by cooks. This recipe demonstrates "papillote," a technique where the bass is seasoned, wrapped in parchment and baked.

Have your fishmonger fillet the fish down to the tail, removing the backbone. This way the fish still has the presence of being whole without the hassle of dealing with bones.

1. Preheat oven to 350 degrees.
2. Cut four 20 x 12 inch parchment sheets.
3. Lay the sheets out in front of you. Place half a tablespoon extra virgin olive oil on each sheet of parchment, [1]. Lay the bass on top of the oil.
4. Open the fish and season with the lemon zest, salt, white pepper and thyme, [2]. Lay top fillet back down and season the top with the remaining oil.
5. Fold the parchment in half to cover the fish, [3]. Start at a side and roll the paper tightly around the fish. Go completely around the fish making sure the roll is tight, [4].

6. Place the 4 papillotes on two sheet pans and place in the oven. Bake for 10 minutes; papillotes will puff with steam when they are close to being done.
7. While the fish is in the oven, place a large sauté pan over medium heat and add the butter.
8. When the butter starts to melt, add the haricots verts and edamame and cook for 3 minutes. When the beans are hot, add the tomatoes, chives, and Lemon Butter and incorporate evenly. Turn off the heat and season with salt and pepper to taste.
9. On four serving plates place an equal amount of beans. Place 1 papillote on each plate, [5]. Cut around the fish and pull the top paper back, [6]. Be careful; the steam is very hot. Finish with a few flakes of the Maldon sea salt.

YIELDS 4 SERVINGS

GRILLED SWORDFISH
WITH CONFIT POTATOES, ARTICHOKES AND LEMON BUTTER

ARTICHOKES
3 lemons, juiced
4 cups water
4 medium artichokes
¼ cup extra virgin olive oil

¼ cup diced onion
¼ cup diced carrots
1 bouquet garni (basil, thyme, and tarragon)
½ cup white wine
2 tablespoons salt

½ teaspoon white pepper

POTATO CONFIT
1 pound fingerling potatoes, washed and scrubbed
2 cups extra virgin olive oil

When we first opened Cypress in 2001, we did not serve swordfish due to the over-fishing of the species. Happily, through the efforts of the Billfish Foundation and other sustainable seafood groups, the population has been renewed and we can feature this popular fish once again.

The artichokes and the potatoes can be prepared a couple of days in advance; they actually taste best when the flavors have had a day or so to marry. Artichokes oxidize quickly and soaking them in the lemon juice retards this process. Also, I recommend that you wear latex gloves to help prevent the artichokes from turning your hands black.

FOR THE ARTICHOKES (SEE ACCOMPANIMENTS P. 204-5 FOR PHOTOS):
1. In a mixing bowl, combine lemon juice and water.
2. Peel away the outer leaves of the artichokes. Lay the artichokes on a cutting board, and cut the top of the artichoke where the leaves start to change from yellow to green, about 1 inch from the base. Peel the stems and trim away the firm green skin. Place the artichokes in the lemon water.

3. In a saucepan, combine the olive oil, onion and carrots. Place over medium heat and sweat for 4 minutes.
4. Add the artichokes and the lemon water to the saucepan along with the bouquet garni, white wine, salt and pepper.
5. Bring to a low simmer and cook for 35 minutes. Artichokes should be fork tender.
6. Remove from heat and allow to cool in the liquid. Remove the bouquet garni. If you are using the artichokes immediately, proceed; if not, place in the refrigerator.
7. Slice the artichokes in half and remove the thistle in the center with a spoon. Place the artichokes back in the liquid with the onions and carrots.
8. To reheat, place the artichokes, carrots and onion in a saucepan over medium heat. This will take about 5 minutes. Artichokes should be warm through. Season the liquid with salt and white pepper, if needed.

1 bulb garlic, cut in half
6 sprigs thyme

GRILLED SWORDFISH
3 tablespoons olive oil

1 teaspoon lemon zest
4 (6-ounce) swordfish steaks (2 inches thick)
Salt
White pepper
4 tablespoons Lemon Butter, cut into coins (see
   p. 25)

12 chervil leaves
Maldon sea salt
Basil Oil (see p. 24)

FOR THE POTATO CONFIT:

1. Preheat oven to 275 degrees.
2. In a small roasting pan, add all the ingredients. The potatoes must be completely submerged in oil.
3. Place a tight lid on the pan or wrap the pan with aluminum foil.
4. Place the pan in the oven for 2 hours. Potatoes should be fork tender when done.
5. Allow the potatoes to cool in the oil.
6. When potatoes are cool, slice into coins 1/2 inch thick.
7. When reheating, warm through in the oil.

FOR THE GRILLED SWORDFISH:

1. Prepare your grill, if using one. You can set it up with medium-high heat.
2. This is also a good time to reheat the potatoes and artichokes.
3. In a mixing bowl, combine the olive oil and lemon zest and incorporate evenly.
4. Coat the swordfish with this oil and season with salt and pepper.
5. Place the swordfish on the grill and cook for 3 minutes on each side. The swordfish should be cooked three-fourths of the way.
6. Remove from the grill and place on a clean plate. Top each piece of swordfish with a coin of lemon butter and let rest 2 minutes. The butter will slightly melt.
7. In four serving bowls, place equal amounts of sliced potatoes, two pieces of artichokes and equal amounts of the diced vegetables. Place a small amount of the artichoke liquid in the bowls and garnish with 4 chervil leaves. Place a piece of grilled swordfish topped with 1 tablespoon Lemon Butter on the potatoes and artichokes. Finish with a sprinkle of Maldon sea salt and a drizzle of Basil Oil.

YIELDS 4 SERVINGS

SZECHWAN PEPPER CRUSTED TUNA
WITH JERUSALEM ARTICHOKES, MIZUNA, BRAISED BELGIAN ENDIVE, CAPERS AND FETA

BRAISED BELGIAN ENDIVE
4 heads Belgian endive, split in half
2 tablespoons extra virgin olive oil
½ cup balsamic vinegar
¼ cup water
1 tablespoon preserved lemon, minced (just the rind used)
1 teaspoon salt
Pinch white pepper

JERUSALEM ARTICHOKES
1 pound Jerusalem artichokes, washed and small knobs removed
Olive oil
2 teaspoons salt
Pinch white pepper

MIZUNA AND CAPERS
1½ cups mizuna greens, cleaned and washed
2 tablespoons capers, rinsed and soaked in water
4 ounces feta cheese, crumbled

2 tablespoons extra virgin olive oil
Salt
White pepper

SZECHWAN TUNA
4 (6-ounce) pieces sashimi tuna, cut in the shapes of rectangles
3 tablespoons Szechwan peppercorns, pulsed in a spice grinder
2 teaspoons salt
3 tablespoons olive oil
Aged Balsamic

Szechwan Pepper is of Chinese origin and imparts a unique "menthol" flavor, as opposed to the heat of traditional peppercorns; it's a good combination with the grilled tuna. Jerusalem Artichokes have the flavor of an artichoke and the skin of a potato. They are related to the sunflower family and are also known as "Sunchokes." (Note: The Jerusalem artichokes can be baked at the same time the Belgian endive is roasting.)

FOR THE BRAISED BELGIAN ENDIVE:
1. Preheat oven to 350 degrees.
2. Remove the core of the Belgian endive, using a melon baller. This part is very tough.
3. Rub the Belgian endive with the olive oil and place in a small roasting pan, cut side down.
4. Cover with the vinegar, water, preserved lemon, salt and pepper.
5. Place in the oven and cook for 35 minutes. Belgian endive should be soft when pierced with a knife and have a caramelized bottom.
6. Cover with a lid or wrap tightly with foil to keep warm.

FOR THE JERUSALEM ARTICHOKES:
1. Preheat oven to 350 degrees.
2. Rub the artichoke with the olive oil, salt and pepper. Place in a roasting pan and bake for 35 minutes. The artichokes should pierce easily with a fork when done.
3. Remove from oven and allow to cool until you can work with them by hand.
4. Slice the artichokes in 1/4-inch coins. When sliced, place them back in the pan to reheat later.

FOR THE MIZUNA AND CAPERS:
1. In a mixing bowl, toss the mizuna with the capers, feta cheese, olive oil and season with salt and pepper.
2. Have this ready when the tuna comes off of the grill.

FOR THE SZECHWAN TUNA:
1. Prepare your grill, if using one. You can set it up with high heat, since the tuna will not be getting cooked long.
2. In a mixing bowl, rub the tuna with the pepper, salt and olive oil. Press the peppercorns into the tuna if they don't want to stick.
3. Before grilling the tuna, place the Belgian Endive and Jerusalem Artichokes back in the oven to get hot.
4. Grill the tuna for 1 minute on each side. Make sure each side is cooked evenly.
5. Once tuna has been grilled, place on a clean pan and transfer to a cutting board.
6. Slice each piece of tuna into thirds.
7. Remove the Belgian Endive and Jerusalem Artichokes from the oven.
8. On four serving plates, place equal amounts of the Jerusalem Artichokes. Place two pieces of Belgian Endive on each place, cut side up. Toss liquid left from the Belgian endive with the mizuna and place equal amounts on the plates. Finish with sliced tuna and a drizzle of Aged Balsamic.

YIELDS 4 SERVINGS

{ P O U L T R Y 6 A N D F O W L }

the recipes

Miso Chicken with Maitake Mushrooms, Green Beans
and Soy Caramel

Maple-Lacquered Quail with Butternut Squash
Risotto and Shallot Pecan Jus

Lemon-Rosemary Roasted Chicken

Pan-Roasted Chicken with Roasted Beets, Baby
Artichokes, and Blood Orange Vinaigrette

Magret Duck Au Poivre with Baby Bok Choy and
Truffle Sweet Potatoes

Smoked Turkey with Bacon Braised Greens and
Natural Jus

Successfully serving poultry in a five-star restaurant is accomplished with the best-quality birds and unique accompaniments. There is no doubt that free-range birds have superior flavor. We purchase our chickens from Belle & Evans and Ashley Farms (see source guide for details). The same goes for turkeys! Cypress flavors such as the Blood Orange Vinaigrette with the Pan-Seared Chicken take these tasty birds to the next level. Never have an ordinary chicken again!

MISO CHICKEN
WITH MAITAKE MUSHROOMS, GREEN BEANS AND SOY CARAMEL

SOY CARAMEL

½ cup soy sauce

¼ cup mirin

3 tablespoons sugar

1 teaspoon orange zest

6 ounces cold butter, cut into pieces

MISO CHICKEN

4 chicken breasts (frenched wing bone)

Salt

White pepper

¼ cup white miso paste

3 tablespoons honey

4 tablespoons canola oil

2 tablespoons butter

3 tablespoons peanut oil

1½ cups Maitake mushrooms (pull into small clusters)

¼ cup Chili Soy (see p. 22)

2 tablespoons butter

8 ounces haricots verts, trimmed and blanched

Salt

White pepper

The Maitake mushrooms and rich Soy Caramel sauce elevate chicken to take center stage in this simple entrée.

FOR THE SOY CARAMEL:

1. In a small saucepan, combine the soy, mirin, sugar and orange zest. Place the saucepan over medium-high heat and reduce liquid by half.

2. Drop the temperature to low and slowly stir in the cold butter, piece by piece.

3. Strain the butter and keep in a warm location.

FOR THE MISO CHICKEN:

1. Season chicken with salt and pepper. In a mixing bowl, combine the miso paste and honey. Mix chicken with miso paste mixture and wrap tightly and refrigerate overnight.

2. Preheat oven to 350 degrees.

3. Place a large nonstick sauté pan over medium-high heat.

Add canola oil and allow to get hot. Add chicken breast, skin side down, and allow to caramelize for 3 minutes.

4. Flip the chicken breast over and cook for another 3 minutes.

5. Add butter and transfer pan to the oven and cook 6 minutes.

6. Check the chicken for doneness. If using an instant-read thermometer, chicken should be 160 degrees. Remove chicken from pan and allow to rest in a warm area.

7. Place a sauté pan over high heat. Add peanut oil and allow pan to get hot. Add mushrooms and caramelize for 2 minutes. Flip mushrooms and add Chili Soy. Reduce soy by half, approximately 2 minutes. Remove from heat and keep warm.

8. Place a large sauté pan over medium heat and add butter. When melted, add haricots verts. Cook for 2 minutes. Season with salt and pepper to taste.

9. On four serving plates, place equal amounts of haricots verts and mushrooms. Place the chicken breast on top of the mushrooms. Finish with Soy Caramel around the chicken.

YIELDS 4 SERVINGS

MAPLE-LACQUERED QUAIL
WITH BUTTERNUT SQUASH RISOTTO AND SHALLOT PECAN JUS

8 semi-boneless quail (wing tips removed and kept for sauce)
1 tablespoon Chinese 5 Spice (see p. 23)
½ tablespoon chopped sage
2 teaspoons salt
2 tablespoons olive oil
¼ cup canola oil
4 tablespoons maple syrup
2 tablespoons butter
Chive Oil (see p. 24)

SHALLOT PECAN JUS
16 quail wing tips
2 cups Duck Stock (see p. 33)
1 tablespoon butter
2 tablespoons thinly sliced shallots
1 tablespoon shaved garlic
1 teaspoon minced sage
1 tablespoon maple syrup
¼ cup toasted pecan halves
Salt
White pepper

BUTTERNUT SQUASH RISOTTO
4 cups water
4 tablespoons olive oil
2 tablespoons minced shallots
2 tablespoons minced garlic
2 cups carniroli or arborio rice
¼ cup white wine
1 cup diced butternut squash
1 teaspoon nutmeg, grated on microplane
¼ cup mascarpone
Salt
White pepper
2 tablespoons minced chives

We have many lowcountry hunters who dine at Cypress and who always appreciate a good quail recipe. If you don't have a freezer full of birds, farm-raised quail are available from Plantation Quail in south Georgia. Take care not to overcook the small birds, as they can be dry.

1. In a mixing bowl, combine quail, Chinese 5 Spice, sage, salt and olive oil; incorporate evenly. Quail should be coated well with the rub.
2. Place two sauté pans over medium-high heat. Divide canola oil between the two pans.
3. Add 4 quail to each pan, breast side down and sear for 2 minutes. Quail should be golden brown. Flip the quail over; drop the temperature to medium-low heat and cook for 3 minutes.
4. Add 2 tablespoons maple syrup to each sauté pan and cook quail evenly with syrup 1 minute. Add 1 tablespoon butter to each pan and baste the quail with both butter and maple syrup.
5. On four serving plates, place an equal amount of risotto and 2 quail per plate. Finish with Shallot Pecan Jus and garnish with Chive Oil.

FOR THE SHALLOT PECAN JUS:
1. Preheat oven to 350 degrees.
2. Place wing tips on a sheet pan in the oven and roast for 10 minutes.
3. Place stock in a small saucepan. Place over medium heat and bring to a simmer.
4. Add wing tips to the stock and reduce by half, approximately 30 minutes.
5. Place a small saucepan over medium-high heat. Add butter, shallots and garlic. Cook for 4 minutes or until caramelized. Add sage and maple syrup and remove from heat.
6. Strain reduced quail stock and add to the saucepan of shallots and garlic. Add the pecan halves and season with salt and pepper.
7. Bring to a simmer and skim off any fat or scum. Lower the heat and keep warm.

FOR THE BUTTERNUT SQUASH RISOTTO:
1. Place water in a small saucepan and bring to a simmer over medium heat.
2. Place a large saucepan over medium heat and add olive oil, shallots and garlic. Cook for 3 minutes. Shallots and garlic should be translucent.
3. Add the rice and stir with shallots and garlic and cook for another 3 minutes. The rice should be golden and smell nutty.
4. Add white wine to the rice and cook for 1 minute, stirring constantly.
5. Slowly add 1/4 cup hot water to the rice, stirring constantly from this point out. Continue to add water 1/4 cup at a time every 2 to 3 minutes. After 1 1/2 cups of water has been added, add the squash. Stir in 1/2 cup water and continue to cook 2 to 3 minutes, stirring constantly. Add another 1/2 cup of water. Stir in grated nutmeg and mascarpone, and season to taste with salt and pepper. If the risotto has a slight bite to it, add another 1/4 cup water and continue to stir. Risotto should be creamy and firm when done.
6. Stir in chives directly before serving risotto and add remaining water if the risotto is tight.

YIELDS 4 SERVINGS

LEMON-ROSEMARY ROASTED CHICKEN

2 (3½-pound) whole chickens	4 sprigs rosemary	White pepper
4 tablespoons Lemon Confit and pulp (see p. 27)	4 tablespoons chopped rosemary	1 teaspoon finely chopped rosemary
4 tablespoons olive oil	Salt	4 tablespoons Lemon Butter (see p. 25)

This is one of the best ways to roast a whole chicken. I recommend that you truss the chicken if possible; it's not difficult, and it allows the bird to cook more evenly. I recommend serving this chicken with a potato gratin and caramelized Brussels sprouts.

1. Preheat oven to 375 degrees.
2. Wash the chickens inside and out and pat dry.
3. Mix Lemon Confit and olive oil and press through a fine sieve. Save both the lemons and the pulp.
4. Place pressed Lemon Confit and 2 sprigs rosemary inside the cavity of each chicken.
5. Truss a chicken with 1 piece of butcher's twine 3 feet long. Place the chicken breast side up with the neck facing you. Push the wing tips under the back bone. Loop the butchers twine around the hind legs and create an X, pulling right over left. Pull tightly between legs and thighs toward the front of the bird. Overlap the wing bone, and tie both pieces around the neck. Repeat the process with the second chicken.
6. In a large roasting pan, place the trussed chickens 2 inches apart. Rub the skin with olive oil-lemon pulp and chopped rosemary, [1]. Shower the chicken with salt. Sprinkle with a light dusting of pepper.
7. Place the roasting pan of chickens in the oven and roast for 1 hour and 20 minutes. Check the chicken between the leg and thigh with an instant-read thermometer. The chicken should read 160 degrees. It will carry over as it rests.
8. Remove the chickens from the oven and allow to rest for 20 minutes, [2]. Transfer to a cutting board and remove the butcher's twine.
9. Remove fat from pan and save the juices. Add the chopped rosemary and Lemon Butter to the pan and scrape with the juices. Strain the sauce into a small pot or container and keep warm.
10. Carve the chicken quarters off and place on each of four serving plates. Carve the breasts off and place on top of the quarters. Finish with equal amounts of the chicken jus.

YIELDS 4 SERVINGS

PAN-ROASTED CHICKEN WITH ROASTED BEETS,
BABY ARTICHOKES AND BLOOD ORANGE VINAIGRETTE

BLOOD ORANGE VINAIGRETTE
¼ cup blood orange juice

¼ cup sherry vinegar

1 tablespoon minced shallots

2 tablespoons honey

2 tablespoons extra virgin olive oil

2 tablespoons Chive Oil (see p. 24)

1½ teaspoons salt

Pinch white pepper

ROASTED BEETS
6 baby beets (golf-ball size), washed, leaves removed

2 tablespoons olive oil

2 tablespoons white wine vinegar

2 teaspoons salt

Pinch white pepper

BABY ARTICHOKES
¼ cup lemon juice

4 cups water

10 cocktail artichokes (about 1 pound)

1 bouquet garni (basil, thyme, and tarragon)

¼ cup white wine

2 tablespoons salt

½ teaspoon white pepper

Colorful and piquant, this chicken recipe is a nice way to show off with exotic blood oranges. The citrus fruits have a deeper flavor than traditional oranges and are commonly available in produce sections during their fall and early-winter season.

FOR THE BLOOD ORANGE VINAIGRETTE:

1. In a small mixing bowl combine all the ingredients and mix evenly.
2. Keep refrigerated. Mix well before using.

FOR THE ROASTED BEETS

1. Preheat oven to 350 degrees.
2. Place the beets on a sheet of aluminum foil and mix with the olive oil, vinegar, salt and pepper. Fold the ends over the beets to form a tight package; make sure there are no openings in the foil.
3. Place the foil package on a sheet tray and bake for 45 minutes. The cooking time depends on the size of the beets: less time for small beets, more time for larger beets. They should be fork tender when done.
4. Remove from oven and allow to cool; make sure you leave the package open. Drain off any juices and save to reheat the beets.
5. Using paper towels, remove the skins from the beets by gently rubbing. I highly recommend wearing gloves for this process.

6. Slice the stem off the beets and cut into quarters.
7. Reheat with the leftover juices and oil before serving.

FOR THE BABY ARTICHOKES

1. In a saucepan combine lemon juice and water.
2. Peel away the outer leaves of the artichokes. Lay the artichokes on a cutting board and cut the top of the artichoke where the leaves start to change from yellow to green, about 1/2 inch from the top. Peel the stems and trim away the firm green skin. Place the artichokes in the lemon water.
3. Add the bouquet garni, white wine, salt and pepper.
4. Place over medium heat and bring to a simmer. Cook for 35 minutes. Artichokes should be fork tender.
5. Remove from heat and allow to cool in the liquid. Remove the bouquet garni. If you are using the artichoke immediately, proceed; if not, place in the refrigerator.
6. Slice the artichokes in half and place the artichokes back in the liquid.
7. To reheat, place the artichokes into a saucepan and place over medium heat. This will take about 5 minutes. Artichokes should be warm through.

Continued on next page

PAN-ROASTED CHICKEN
4 boneless chicken breasts, tenderloin attached
Salt

White pepper
Canola oil
3 tablespoons butter

4 sprigs thyme
1 tablespoon minced chives
4 chive tips

FOR THE PAN-ROASTED CHICKEN

1. Season the chicken breasts with salt and pepper.
2. Place a large sauté pan over medium-high heat and add enough canola oil to cover the bottom of the pan by 1/8 inch. Let the oil get hot.
3. Carefully lay the seasoned chicken breasts skin side down in the pan. Cook for 4 minutes; drop the heat to medium and cook for 5 minutes.
4. Flip the chicken over and cook for 6 minutes. Add the butter and thyme to the pan and baste the chicken with the juices, 2 minutes.

5. The chicken should be cooked. Juices should run clear or be a temperature of 160 degrees on an instant-read thermometer. The chicken will carry over while resting.
6. Remove the chicken from the pan and place on paper towels. Place in a warm area and rest for 5 minutes. Slice the chicken directly before serving.
7. Reheat the Roasted Beets and the Baby Artichokes. Add the minced chives to the vinaigrette and incorporate evenly.
8. On four serving plates, place an equal amount of the beets, artichokes and blood orange vinaigrette. Place the sliced chicken breast on top and garnish with chive tips.

YIELDS 4 SERVINGS

MAGRET DUCK AU POIVRE
WITH BABY BOK CHOY AND TRUFFLE SWEET POTATOES

4 cups water	½ tablespoon salt	Salt
4 tablespoons salt	2 teaspoons chopped sage	White pepper
2 cups Duck Stock (see p. 33)	2 tablespoons oil	4 heads baby bok choy, washed, bottoms removed
2 Magret duck breasts (1 pound each)	¼ cup Grand Marnier	Coarse sea salt
2 tablespoons green peppercorns, rinsed well		

We have foie gras on the menu at Cypress, and in the spirit of using the product to its fullest potential, I feel compelled to serve the duck breast as well. Magret duck breasts are large and robust in flavor. I can even taste a hint of the foie gras in this classic rendition of the bird.

1. In a large pot, combine the water and salt. Place over medium-high heat and bring to a boil.
2. Place the stock in a medium saucepan and reduce by two-thirds over medium heat. When reduced, remove from heat and keep warm.
3. Score the skin of the duck breasts in a small checkerboard pattern, [1]. This will allow the ducks to render evenly and cut down on the length of cooking time.
4. In a spice grinder combine the green peppercorns, salt, sage and oil. Pulse to a fine paste, [2]. Scrap down the sides if needed and pulse again. Mixture should be smooth.
5. Rub the duck breasts meat side only with the rub; make sure it is an even layer.
6. Place a large sauté pan over medium-high heat. Add the duck breasts fat side down, to the sauté pan, [3]. Lightly press the meat down to ensure even cooking. Render the fat out of the duck for 5 minutes. The skin will be brown and crispy when done.
7. Flip the breasts over and cook for 3 minutes while basting the skin with the hot duck fat. The duck should be cooked to a medium doneness.
8. Remove the duck from the pan and place on paper towels to rest in a warm location.
9. To finish the sauce, deglaze the pan with the Grand Marnier. (Do this over low heat; if you have gas it may flame up.) Place the pan back over heat, scraping the caramelized pan with the Grand Marnier. Reduce by half.
10. Add the reduced stock and cook for 1 minute. The sauce should have body. Season with salt and white pepper to taste. Reduce the heat and skim any fat or scum off of the top. Strain through a fine sieve into a small pot and keep warm.
11. Blanch the bok choy in boiling salted water for 30 seconds. Remove from water and place in a bowl lined with paper towels. Using more towels, press lightly to absorb excess water. Remove the towels and season with salt and pepper lightly.
12. Slice the duck into 1/8-inch slices before plating, [4].

Coninued on next page

TRUFFLE SWEET POTATOES

Water

3 pounds sweet potatoes, peeled and cut into ½-inch-thick rounds

1½ tablespoons salt

1 tablespoon honey

4 tablespoons Truffle Butter, cut into pieces (see p. 26)

2 tablespoons salt

1 teaspoon white pepper

13. On four serving plates, place equal amounts of the sweet potatoes in a straight line. Place the bok choy parallel to the sweet potatoes. Lay the sliced duck breast on top of the bok choy. Spoon the green peppercorn sauce over the duck and finish with a few grains of course sea salt.

FOR THE TRUFFLE SWEET POTATOES:

1. In a large pot, add potatoes and salt and cover with water.

2. Place over medium heat and cook for 25 minutes. Potatoes should split when pierced with a fork.

3. Transfer the potatoes to a colander and drain.

4. Place a food mill with the smallest screen over the pot you cooked the potatoes in. Work the hot potatoes through the food mill.

5. Add the honey, Truffle Butter, salt and pepper. Incorporate evenly until the butter is melted.

6. Keep the potatoes in a warm area. If you have a lid, use it, or wrap tightly with food film.

YIELDS 4 SERVINGS

SMOKED TURKEY
WITH BACON BRAISED GREENS AND NATURAL JUS

2 cups water
¾ cup salt
½ cup light brown sugar
3 sprigs sage
4 sprigs thyme
1 bulb garlic, split in half
5 white peppercorns
3 bay leaves

2 gallons ice water
1 (10- to 14-pound) turkey, giblets and neck
    removed

SMOKING AND COOKING THE TURKEY
4 tablespoons olive oil
Salt
White pepper

NATURAL JUS
Turkey bones and wings
Water
½ cup onion, large chop
¾ cup leeks, large chop
¼ cup celery, large chop
¼ cup carrots, large chop
1 garlic bulb, skin removed, cut in half

This is the turkey I make every year for the Cypress staff meal on Thanksgiving. We also serve it with cornbread stuffing and Gruyère Potato Fondue. Since the bird is broken down, the meat is consistently cooked—a nice departure from crispy on the outside, cold on the inside whole turkeys.

The brine is the single most important part of a moist, delicious turkey. When I was a kid, my dad was making the brine while I was skateboarding around the driveway. Inevitably, the skate hit the bucket of brine and knocked it over. I got yelled at for my mistake, but I still did not understand what brine was.

Things run in circles. On Thanksgiving 2005, I had 12 turkeys in a brine and someone accidentally drained them. I caught their goof after an hour and took the staff to task. The episode made me remember my childhood experience and I reflected as to why my dad had been so mad. The brine makes the difference between a good turkey and a great one. This recipe can also be used on whole chickens and pork loins.

1. In a saucepan, combine 2 cups water, salt and sugar. Place over medium-high heat. Stir until salt and sugar are dissolved. If it starts to boil, lower the temperature.
2. Add the sage, thyme, garlic, peppercorns and bay leaves and cook 3 minutes.
3. In a large container, combine the ice water and the hot mixture. Stir with a large spoon. Liquid should be ice cold.
4. Place the turkey into the brine and refrigerate for 24 hours.
5. Remove the turkey from the brine and in a colander with the legs facing down to drain excess brine. Brine can be discarded.
6. Using paper towels, pat the turkey dry.

7. Place the turkey on a cutting board and debone, leaving you with two breasts and two leg quarters, two full wings and the carcass.
8. Using a cleaver, cut the carcass into 6 smaller pieces. Cut the wings into three segments. All of this will be used to make stock.

FOR SMOKING AND COOKING THE TURKEY:
1. Preheat oven to 300 degrees.
2. If you are using a smoker, heat it to 220 degrees. If you are using a grill, set it to the lowest setting on one side and add wood chips. Keep the opposite side turned off.
3. Rub the turkey breasts and quarters with olive oil and season with salt and pepper.
4. Add the breast and leg quarters to your smoker or grill and smoke for 30 minutes. If using a grill, place turkey on the side that is turned off.
5. Remove the turkey from the smoker or grill and place on separate sheet trays, one for the legs and one for the breasts. Wrap the turkey breast and refrigerate until ready to cook.
6. Place the turkey legs in the oven and cook for 1 hour. Add the turkey breast to the oven and cook for 45 minutes. This way, both come out of the oven at the same time.
7. Remove from the oven and let rest 10 minutes.
8. Turn oven temperature down to 180 degrees.
9. Pull the meat off of the legs and place on a tray and keep warm.
10. Slice the turkey breast into 1/4-inch-thick slices and keep warm.
11. Place the turkey in the oven just to keep warm. Only do this if you are not ready to serve.

5 sprigs parsley

2 sprigs sage

4 sprigs thyme

4 bay leaves

10 white peppercorns

Salt

Pepper

3 tablespoons butter

½ tablespoon minced chives

BACON BRAISED GREENS

Water

½ cup salt

2 heads mustard greens, ribs removed, chopped and washed

1 head collard greens, chopped and washed

2 heads escarole, chopped and washed

½ cup bacon, small dice

2 cups julienned onions

2 tablespoons minced garlic

½ cup Smoked Pork Stock (see p. 34)

3 tablespoons salt

½ tablespoon white pepper

3 tablespoons Herb Butter (see p. 26)

FOR THE NATURAL JUS

1. Preheat oven to 350 degrees.

2. Place the turkey bones and wing segments evenly in a roasting pan.

3. Roast the bones for 1 hour. Move the bones around and roast for another 20 minutes. Remove the bones from the oven; add the bones to a large stockpot (16 quart or larger). Pour off the fat. Deglaze the pan by adding 2 cups of water to the pan. Place back in the oven for 3 to 4 minutes, then remove the pan and scrape the bottom with a metal spatula to loosen the fond. Add this to the stockpot.

4. Cover the bones with cold water. Add the onion, leeks, celery, carrots and garlic to the stockpot. Top off the mirepoix with the parsley, sage, thyme, bay leaves and peppercorns.

5. Place stockpot over medium heat and bring to a simmer. As the water begins to simmer, a scum will start to form at the top, this needs to be removed. Pull the stockpot slightly off the heat; this will allow a slow convective movement that moves the scum to one side of the pot for easy removal. Continue skimming frequently. Cook the stock for 3 hours.

6. Turn off the heat to the stockpot and allow it to cool slowly. Strain the stock through a fine sieve into another large stockpot. Place the stockpot with the stock in it back on the stove over medium heat and bring to a simmer. Continue to skim the scum and fat off of the top.

7. Reduce the stock by three-fourths; this will take about 3 hours. The stock should have a light body.

8. When the stock is reduced, season to taste with salt and pepper.

9. Using an immersion blender, add the butter.

10. Finish with the chives.

FOR THE BACON BRAISED GREENS

1. Fill a large stockpot three-fourths full of water and add the salt. Place over high heat and bring to a boil. Fill a large bowl half full with ice water.

2. When the water is boiling, blanch the mustard greens in two batches for 1 minute per batch. Remove from water and shock in the ice water.

3. Allow the water to return to a boil and repeat the process with the collard greens, extending the cook time to 3 minutes. Shock in the ice water.

4. Allow the water to return to a boil and repeat the process with the escarole and cook for 1 minute. Shock in the ice water.

5. When all the greens have been blanched, remove from the bowl and place in a colander to drain. Press down on the greens, removing as much water as possible.

6. Place a large saucepan over medium heat and add diced bacon. Render the bacon for 5 minutes. Bacon should be lightly caramelized.

7. Add the onions and garlic and cook for 5 minutes. Onions will be translucent.

8. Add the greens to the pan and incorporate evenly.

9. Add the stock, salt and pepper and stir in the herb butter.

10. When the greens are hot and mixed evenly, remove from heat.

11. Cover with a lid and keep warm.

YIELDS 4 SERVINGS

{ M E A T S }

7

the recipes

Roast Pork Shoulder with Choucroute and Gruyère Potato Fondue

Châteaubriand with Château Potatoes, Haricots Verts, Béarnaise and Madeira Sauces

Grilled Filet of Beef with Boursin Cheese, Asparagus, Fingerling Potatoes and Madeira Sauce

Coriander Pork with Caramelized Fennel and Raisin Caper Compote

Steak Diane with Roasted Mushrooms, Gruyère Potato Fondue and Truffle Cracked Peppercorn Cream

Thai-Spiced Short Rib and Lobster with Edamame, Shiitake Mushrooms, Teardrop Tomatoes and Celery Root Purée

Veal Oscar with Asparagus, Crispy Soft-shell Crab and Béarnaise

Deconstructed Lamb T-Bone with English Pea Risotto

Garlic and Herb Roasted Rack of Lamb with Château Potatoes, Haricots Verts and Balsamic Lamb Reduction

Braised Lamb Shanks with Roquefort Polenta and Roasted Beets

Cypress's meat entrées are the best of old and new. Classic cuts, old world recipes and tableside presentations are updated with new ingredients and, as always, our signature Asian flavors and seasonal elements.

When choosing meats, I prefer more challenging cuts like shanks and shoulders, as the flavors are deeper than a quickly cooked tenderloin. Techniques such as braising, slow roasting and smoking work well with these cuts, producing deliciously complex layers of flavors.

ROAST PORK SHOULDER
WITH CHOUCROUTE AND GRUYÈRE POTATO FONDUE

CHOUCROUTE

1 pound sauerkraut, drained

4 ounces slab bacon

2 links bratwurst (half a pound)

1 tablespoon salt

1½ teaspoons white pepper

1 (12-ounce) lager beer (Yuengling
recommended)

PORK SHOULDER

1 (3-pound) boneless pork shoulder (can
substitute Boston Butt or picnic ham)

2 tablespoons kosher salt

½ tablespoon white pepper

½ pound caul fat

4 tablespoons butter

Gruyère Potato Fondue (see p. 206)

This recipe is an updated version of my mother's traditional New Year's Day meal. Mom put up her own sauerkraut (fermented cabbage and salt), which I see as the northern equivalent of the south's beloved collard greens.

FOR THE CHOUCROUTE:

1. Preheat oven to 325 degrees.

2. In a roasting pan, combine sauerkraut, bacon, bratwurst, salt, pepper and beer. Cover tightly with aluminum foil and place in oven. Cook for 1 1/2 hours.

3. Remove from oven. Pull bacon and bratwurst out of the sauerkraut and cut both into 8 pieces. Place back in sauerkraut and keep warm.

FOR THE PORK SHOULDER:

1. Preheat oven to 220 degrees.

2. In a large mixing bowl, combine salt and pepper; incorporate evenly. Rub the pork shoulder with the mixture until evenly coated.

3. Place pork shoulder in a roasting pan.

4. Place shoulder in the oven and bake for 10 hours. Meat should pull apart, or you can check it with an instant-read thermometer of 180 degrees.

5. Remove from oven and let rest for 30 minutes at room temperature.

6. Pull pork into small pieces. Discard any pieces of fat.

7. Place the pulled pork into an 8 x 8 inch baking pan. Place another 8 x 8 inch pan on top and weigh down with a heavy object. Press tightly for 20 minutes. Remove weight and refrigerate overnight.

8. Preheat oven to 350 degrees.

9. Remove pork from baking pan and cut into 4-inch square blocks.

10. Place the caul fat on a cutting board. Place a pork block on top of the caul fat and roll around pork tightly. Fold in the ends and trim the caul fat. Repeat for the remaining pork blocks.

11. Place the wrapped blocks on a greased sheet pan. Place 1 tablespoon butter on top of each piece and bake for 12 minutes, or until the outsides are crispy and brown.

12. On four serving plates, place a round circle of Gruyère Potato Fondue. Place equal amounts of sauerkraut, bacon and bratwurst inside the ring of potato. Top with a block of crispy pork.

YIELDS 4 SERVINGS

CHÂTEAUBRIAND WITH CHÂTEAU POTATOES,
HARICOTS VERTS, BÉARNAISE AND MADEIRA SAUCES

2½ pounds beef tenderloin, center cut, tied
Salt
Black pepper
4 tablespoons olive oil
2 tablespoons butter
1 pound haricots verts, trimmed and blanched
White pepper

Madeira Sauce (see p. 175)
Béarnaise Sauce (see p. 189)

CHÂTEAU POTATOES
20 red bliss potatoes (golf-ball size)
Water

3 tablespoons salt
2 sprigs thyme
Canola oil
2 tablespoons butter
Salt
White pepper

Literally translated, "Châteaubriand" refers to a beef entrée to serve two people. This recipe uses a center cut piece of beef—the full tenderloin, without the head and tail. Château potatoes are trimmed to look like large olives. Béarnaise is the classic sauce. Tiny green beans and the Madeira sauce put the Cypress stamp on it.

FOR THE CHÂTEAUBRIAND:

1. Prepare your grill, if using one. You can set it up with medium-high heat.
2. Season the beef with salt, black pepper and olive oil. Leave at room temperature for 25 minutes.
3. Place the meat on the grill and cook for 2 minutes, [1].
4. Continue cooking the meat for approximately 15 minutes (for medium-rare) rolling from side to side.
5. Remove the meat from the grill and place on a clean tray. Place in a warm location and let rest for 10 minutes.
6. Place a large sauté pan over medium heat and add the butter. When butter is melted, add the haricots verts and cook 2 minutes. Season with salt and white pepper to taste; keep warm.
7. Remove the butcher's twine from the beef and place the meat on a cutting board, [2].

8. Slice the meat into 8 even pieces.
9. On four serving plates, place 5 chateau potatoes and an equal amount of haricots verts. Place 2 slices of meat on each plate and finish with Béarnaise Sauce over the meat and Madeira Sauce around the plate.

FOR THE CHÂTEAU POTATOES:

1. Trim the potatoes into equal-size football shapes, [3].
2. Place the potatoes in a saucepan and cover with water. Add the salt and thyme and place over medium heat to simmer for 12 minutes. Potatoes should have a slightly firm center when pierced with a knife.
3. Remove potatoes from heat and carefully place in a colander to drain.
4. Place a large sauté pan over medium-high heat and add a thin layer of oil to the pan. When oil is hot, add the potatoes to the pan. Cook for 3 minutes, and roll the potatoes around so they brown evenly. Add the butter to the pan and roll the potatoes around again. Season with salt and pepper. Potatoes should be fork tender.
5. Remove the potatoes from the pan and place on paper towels to absorb excess grease. Keep warm.

YIELDS 4 SERVINGS

GRILLED FILET OF BEEF
WITH BOURSIN CHEESE, ASPARAGUS, FINGERLING POTATOES AND MADEIRA SAUCE

MADEIRA SAUCE

YIELDS 1 CUP

3 cups Veal Stock (see p. 31)

1 cup Madeira wine

2 tablespoons minced shallots

½ tablespoon minced garlic

2 sprigs thyme

Salt

White pepper

BOURSIN

3 tablespoons butter

¼ cup diced shallots

3 tablespoons minced garlic

1 cup julienned spinach

1½ teaspoons chopped thyme

1½ teaspoons chopped basil

1 teaspoon salt

1 teaspoon white pepper

1 pound cream cheese

2 tablespoons Parmesan cheese

¼ cup Danish blue cheese

4 tablespoons goat cheese (fromage blanc)

ROASTED FINGERLING POTATOES

2 tablespoons olive oil

1 pound fingerling potatoes, cut in half

Salt

White pepper

2 sprigs thyme

1 tablespoon butter

FOR THE MADEIRA SAUCE:

1. Place the stock in a saucepan. Place over medium heat and cook for about an hour. Sauce should be reduced by two-thirds. Skim the stock as needed.

2. Add the Madeira, shallots, garlic and thyme to a saucepan and bring to a simmer. Reduce by three-fourths. Add this to the reduced stock.

3. Simmer the sauce and season with salt and pepper to taste. Strain the sauce through a fine sieve into a small saucepan and keep warm.

FOR THE BOURSIN:

1. Place a sauté pan over medium heat. Add the butter. When melted, add the shallots and garlic. Stir often while cooking for 5 minutes. Mixture should be lightly caramelized.

2. Remove the pan from heat and fold in the spinach, herbs, salt and pepper. Allow to cool.

3. Using a mixer, cream together the cream cheese, Parmesan cheese, blue cheese and goat cheese. Mixture should be smooth and creamy.

4. Using a rubber spatula, fold the spinach into the cheese mixture until incorporated evenly.

5. Place in a container and refrigerate for up to 1 week.

FOR THE ROASTED POTATOES:

1. Preheat oven to 350 degrees.

2. Place a large sauté pan over medium heat and add the oil.

3. Add the potatoes, season with salt and pepper and cook for 2 minutes. Remove from heat and place in the oven for 30 minutes. Potatoes should be fork tender.

4. Remove the pan from the oven and add the thyme and butter and baste the potatoes with the butter.

5. Place the potatoes on a plate lined with paper towels to absorb excess grease; keep warm.

Continued on next page

SAUTÉED ASPARAGUS

2 tablespoons butter

1 pound asparagus, trimmed and blanched

4 tablespoons water

Salt

White pepper

GRILLED FILET OF BEEF

4 (8-ounce) beef tenderloins

Salt

Black pepper

4 tablespoons olive oil

FOR THE ASPARAGUS

1. Place a sauté pan over medium heat and add the butter.

2. Add the asparagus and cook 3 minutes, while moving asparagus frequently. Add the salt and pepper to taste. Keep warm.

FOR THE FILET OF BEEF

1. Preheat broiler to low.

2. Prepare your grill if using one. You can set it up with medium-high heat.

3. Season the beef with salt and pepper and olive oil. Leave at room temperature for 25 minutes.

4. Place the meat on the grill and cook for 3 minutes. Flip the meat and cook for another 3 minutes. If the filets are thick, roll on their sides and cook sides evenly.

5. Continue cooking the meat for 2 minutes, flipping from side to side every 30 seconds.

6. Remove the meat from the grill and place on a clean tray. Place in a warm location and rest meat for 5 minutes.

7. Place 1 1/2 tablespoons of Boursin on top of each filet. Place under the broiler for 30 seconds, just to melt the tops of the cheese.

8. On four serving plates, place equal amounts of sautéed asparagus. Place the filet on top of the asparagus and the potatoes behind the filet. Finish with 2 tablespoons Madeira sauce.

YIELDS 4 SERVINGS

CORIANDER PORK
WITH CARAMELIZED FENNEL AND RAISIN CAPER COMPOTE

RAISIN CAPER COMPOTE

¼ cup golden raisins

¼ cup white wine vinegar

¼ cup water

3 tablespoons capers, rinsed well

2 tablespoons julienned shallots

1 tablespoon garlic, mandolin shaved

1 teaspoon lemon zest

1½ teaspoons salt

Pinch white pepper

1 teaspoon chopped chervil

1 teaspoon chopped mint

CARAMELIZED FENNEL

1 large bulb fennel, trimmed to bulb only
    (saving a few fronds for garnish)

1 large onion, peeled and cut in half

¼ cup extra virgin olive oil

½ tablespoon salt

½ teaspoon white pepper

½ teaspoon lemon zest

3 tablespoons Lemon Butter (see p. 25)

CORIANDER PORK

3 tablespoons coriander seed

2 teaspoons salt

1 teaspoon white pepper

3 tablespoons olive oil

4 boneless pork loins, cut 2 inches thick (1½ to 2
    pounds total weight)

Canola oil

3 tablespoons butter

Extra virgin olive oil

Fennel fronds (saved from the fennel tops)

Mediterranean flavors shine through in this recipe. If you do not like raisins, you may substitute fresh grapes as an alternative.

FOR THE RAISIN CAPER COMPOTE:

1. In a small, nonreactive container combine the raisins, vinegar and water. Let sit overnight to plump the raisins.
2. Add the remaining ingredients to the plump raisins and incorporate evenly.
3. Mixture can be refrigerated for 1 day.

FOR THE CARAMELIZED FENNEL:

1. Cut the fennel in half and remove the core. Slice the fennel into 1/4-inch slices.
2. Remove the core of the onion and slice the same thickness as the fennel.
3. Place a large pan over medium-high heat. When hot, add the olive oil, fennel and onion and cook for 5 minutes. Lower the temperature to medium and cook another 5 minutes. The onion and fennel should be soft and caramelized.
4. Season with salt, pepper, and lemon zest; incorporate evenly.
5. Remove from heat and place in a warm location. Reheat before serving if needed.
6. Stir in the Lemon Butter directly before serving.

FOR THE CORIANDER PORK:

1. Place the coriander seeds in a spice grinder and pulse fine.
2. Add the coriander to a mixing bowl and add salt, pepper, and olive oil; incorporate evenly.
3. Add the pieces of pork to the bowl and rub with the coriander evenly.
4. Allow to sit for 20 minutes. (Do not refrigerate.)
5. Place a large sauté pan over medium-high heat and add enough canola oil to cover the bottom of the pan by 1/8 inch. Let the oil get hot.
6. Carefully lay the rubbed pork in the pan. Cook for 2 minutes.
7. Flip the pork over and cook for 2 minutes. Drop the temperature to medium-low and cook, flipping the pork every minute, for 3 minutes. Add the butter to the pan and baste the pork with the juices, 2 minutes.
8. The pork should be cooked medium or be at a temperature of 145 degrees on an instant-read thermometer.
9. Remove the pork from the pan and place on paper towels. Place in a warm area and rest for 5 minutes. Slice the pork into 1/4-inch-thick slices before serving.
10. On four serving plates, place equal amounts of the Caramelized Fennel. Place the sliced pork on top of the fennel. Place an equal amount of the Raisin Caper Compote on top of the pork. Garnish with extra virgin olive oil and fennel fronds.

YIELDS 4 SERVINGS

STEAK DIANE WITH ROASTED MUSHROOMS,
GRUYÈRE POTATO FONDUE AND TRUFFLE CRACKED PEPPERCORN CREAM

2 (1-pound) New York strip steaks (2½ inches thick)
Salt
Black pepper
Canola oil
3 tablespoons Herb Butter (see p. 26)
8 sprigs thyme
Gruyère Potato Fondue (see p. 206)

TRUFFLE CRACKED PEPPERCORN CREAM
2 tablespoons olive oil

2 tablespoons diced shallots
½ tablespoon minced garlic
1½ teaspoons cracked black pepper
¼ cup red wine
1½ tablespoons Dijon mustard
3 cups Veal Stock (see p. 31)
1 sprig thyme
1 tablespoon chopped truffle
3 tablespoons heavy cream
Salt

ROASTED MUSHROOMS
8 ounces cremini mushrooms
2 large portobello mushrooms, stems removed
8 ounces shiitake mushrooms, stems removed
4 tablespoons olive oil
½ tablespoon salt
1 teaspoon white pepper
2 tablespoons Herb Butter (see p. 26)

Truffles and sharp cracked peppercorns update the decadent sauce for this old world classic.

1. Season steak with salt and pepper. If meat is cold, allow to sit at room temperature for 25 minutes.
2. Place a large sauté pan over medium-high heat and add enough canola oil to cover the bottom of the pan by 1/8 inch. Let the oil get hot.
3. Carefully lay the steaks in the pan. Cook for 2 minutes.
4. Flip the steaks over and cook for 2 minutes more. Drop the temperature to medium-low and cook, flipping the steaks every minute, for 4 minutes. Add the Herb Butter and thyme to the pan and baste the steaks for 2 minutes.
5. The steaks should be cooked medium-rare.
6. Remove the steaks from the pan and place on paper towels. Place in a warm area and rest for 5 minutes. Slice the steaks into 1/4-inch-thick slices before serving.
7. On four serving plates, place equal amounts of potatoes in the center. Using a kitchen spoon, press down on the potatoes and drag spoon. This will create a well where you will place an equal amount of mushrooms. Place the steak slices on top of the mushrooms. Place the cream sauce around the plate and serve immediately.

FOR THE TRUFFLE CRACKED PEPPERCORN CREAM:
1. Place a saucepan over medium heat. Add olive oil, shallots, garlic and pepper. Sweat for 3 minutes.

2. Add red wine and reduce to a couple of tablespoons, approximately 5 minutes.
3. Add mustard, stock, and thyme and incorporate evenly. Reduce the sauce by two-thirds. Skim any scum coming to the top. The sauce will take 20 minutes to reduce.
4. Add the chopped truffle and heavy cream and then bring to a simmer. Season with salt to taste.
5. Strain the sauce through a fine sieve into a small pan, cover with a lid or wrap tightly and keep warm.

FOR ROASTED MUSHROOMS:
1. Slice cremini mushrooms into 1/4 inch pieces and place in a mixing bowl.
2. Break up the portobello mushrooms into 1-inch pieces and break the shiitake mushrooms in half and add to the mixing bowl.
3. Place a large sauté pan over medium-high heat. Add olive oil and allow to get hot. Place mushrooms in the pan and cook for 3 minutes. Stir the mushrooms around and cook for another 3 minutes. There should be very little moisture left in the pan.
4. Remove from heat, season with salt and pepper and add Herb Butter.
5. Keep warm.

YIELDS 4 SERVINGS

THAI-SPICED SHORT RIB AND LOBSTER
WITH EDAMAME, SHIITAKE MUSHROOMS, TEARDROP TOMATOES AND CELERY ROOT PURÉE

THAI SPICE

1 cinnamon stick

1 tablespoon star anise

1 tablespoon fenugreek seeds

1 tablespoon Szechwan peppercorn

½ tablespoon dried ginger

CELERY ROOT PURÉE

4 pounds celery root, peeled and cut into cubes

2 tablespoons salt

Water

¾ cup butter, cut into cubes

1½ tablespoons salt

1½ teaspoons white pepper

SHORT RIBS

4 pounds beef short ribs, bones removed

4 tablespoons canola oil

½ cup chopped onion

¼ cup chopped leeks

This is a flavorful (versus spicy) Thai dish, inspired by the fragrant Szechwan peppercorn, cardamom and star anise (used in the Thai spice). The ribs are incredibly tender, with a sauce that is a good alternative to a traditional red wine braise.

FOR THE THAI SPICE:

1. Toast the spices in a small pan over high heat for 30 seconds.
2. Place into a spice grinder and pulse until powder.
3. Place in a tight container for later use.

FOR THE CELERY ROOT PURÉE:

1. In a large pot, add celery root, salt and cover with water.
2. Place over medium heat and cook for 35 minutes. Celery root should split when pierced with a fork.
3. Transfer the celery root to a colander and drain.
4. Place a food mill with the smallest screen over the pot you cooked the celery root in. Work the hot celery root through the food mill.
5. Stir in the butter cubes until melted. The celery root should have a velvety consistency.
6. Season with the salt and pepper; incorporate evenly. Adjust seasoning if needed.
7. Keep the celery root in a warm area. If you have a lid, use it or wrap tightly with food film.

Continued on next page

¼ cup chopped carrot	3 cups Veal Stock (see p. 31)	Salt
¼ cup chopped celery	2 cups water	White pepper
1 bulb garlic, split in half	2 tablespoons canola oil	2 (1–¼ pound) lobsters (see p. 79)
2 sprigs mint	1 cup baby shiitake mushrooms	Beurre Fondue (see p. 113)
2 sprigs cilantro	½ cup edamame	
¼ cup mushroom soy	3/4 cup teardrop tomatoes, cut in half	

FOR THE SHORT RIBS:

1. Preheat oven to 250 degrees.

2. Trim the short ribs of excess fat and season both sides with 2 tablespoons Thai Spice, **[1]**.

3. Place a pot or a roasting pan large enough to hold the short ribs over medium-high heat and add the oil. Let the oil get hot.

4. Add the short ribs to the pan and sear for 5 minutes, **[2]**. Meat will have a crispy crust. Flip and sear opposite side for 5 minutes. Carefully remove the short ribs from the pan and pour off excess fat.

5. Add the onion, leeks, carrot, celery, garlic, mint and cilantro to the pan, **[3]**. Cover with cheesecloth and place the short ribs on top, **[4]**. Add the mushroom soy, stock and water. This should cover the ribs by a little more than half.

6. Cover pot with a tight lid or aluminum foil. Place in oven and cook for 5 hours.

7. When short ribs are done, remove from oven and allow them to cool in the pan. When cool, refrigerate for at least one full day.

8. Preheat oven to 300 degrees.

9. Break fat cap off top layer and remove short ribs. Place on a cutting board and cut into 4 blocks. Keep refrigerated until ready to use.

10. Place pan on the stove over medium-high heat and bring to a simmer. When sauce has returned to a liquid state, strain through a fine sieve into another pan. Discard the vegetables.

11. Place pan back over heat and reduce by two-thirds. Skim fat and scum that rises to the surface. Season with salt and pepper to taste. The sauce should be syrupy.

12. Place the short ribs on a tray and brush Thai sauce over the ribs and add 1/4 cup water to the tray. Place in the oven to heat through 8 to 10 minutes.

13. Place a sauté pan over medium-high heat. Add the canola oil and let it get hot. Add shiitake mushrooms and cook for 3 minutes. Add the edamame and cook for 2 minutes. Remove from heat, add tomatoes and season with salt and pepper. Keep vegetables warm.

14. Add lobster meat to the Beurre Fondue and cook over low heat for 5 minutes.

15. On four serving plates, place Celery Root Purée in the center. Using a kitchen spoon press down on the purée and drag spoon. This will create a well where you will place an equal amount of edamame, shiitake mushrooms and tomatoes. Place a short rib block on top. Place the sauce over the short ribs and top with 1/2 tail and lobster claw.

YIELDS 4 SERVINGS

VEAL OSCAR WITH ASPARAGUS,
CRISPY SOFT-SHELL CRAB AND BÉARNAISE

4 pounds veal breast on the bone (half of a veal
    breast)
Salt
White pepper
4 tablespoons olive oil
½ cup chopped onion
¼ cup chopped leeks
¼ cup chopped carrot
¼ cup chopped celery
1 bulb garlic, split in half
4 sprigs thyme

4 cups Veal Stock (see p. 31)
3 cups water
¼ cup water
Béarnaise (see below)
Sautéed Asparagus (see p. 176)
Coarse sea salt

BÉARNAISE
3 tablespoons white wine vinegar
1 tablespoon minced shallots
2 tablespoons tarragon picked from stem and
    chopped

2 egg yolks
3 tablespoons water
1 tablespoon lemon juice
3/4 cup clarified butter (warm to touch)
Salt
White pepper

TEMPURA SOFT-SHELL CRAB
1 gallon peanut or canola oil
3 soft-shell crabs
Tempura Batter (see p. 133)
Fine sea salt

This recipe is based on a classic dish and is dressed up for the two times out of the year that soft-shell crabs are available (April and September). The veal breast should be braised at least one day in advance for the flavors to marry. It also goes well with the Potato Gratin (see p. 206).

1. Preheat oven to 250 degrees. Trim the veal breast of excess fat and season the meat side with salt and pepper.
2. Place a roasting pan large enough to hold the veal breast over medium-high heat and add the oil. Let the oil get hot.
3. Add the veal to the pan, meat side down, and sear for 5 minutes. Meat will have a crispy crust. Carefully remove the veal from the pan and pour off excess fat.
4. Add the onion, leeks, carrot, celery, garlic and thyme to the pan. Place the veal breast to the top of the mirepoix and add the stock and water. This should cover the veal by a little more than half.
5. Cover pan with a tight lid or aluminum foil. Place in oven and cook for 6 hours.
6. When veal is done, remove from oven and allow to cool in the pan. When cool, refrigerate for a least one full day.
7. Preheat oven to 300 degrees.
8. Break fat cap off top layer in the pan and remove the veal breast. Place the pan on the stove over medium heat and bring to a simmer.
9. Place veal on a cutting board and cut the meat off the bones. (It will be easy to see where to cut; the veal pulls away from the bones as it cooks.) Cut the veal into 6 strips. Keep refrigerated until ready to use.

10. When sauce in pan has returned to a liquid state, strain through a fine sieve into another pan. Discard the vegetables.
11. Place the pan over heat and reduce liquid by two-thirds. Skim fat and scum that rises to the surface. Season with salt and pepper to taste. The sauce should be syrupy.

FOR THE BÉARNAISE:

1. In a small saucepan add the vinegar and shallots. Place over medium low heat and reduce by 3/4. Add the tarragon and keep warm.
2. In a small mixing bowl combine the egg yolks, water, and lemon juice.
3. Place the bowl over a simmering pot of water or place over a low heat flame and whisk continuously. The mixture will double in volume and will start to steam. Steam is good; it is the water cooking out.
4. The eggs will become tight as they cook. When they are fully cooked, you will see ribbons form after the whisk moves through the eggs. The eggs should taste cooked when done.
5. Remove the bowl from heat and place on a towel to keep the bowl from moving.
6. Slowly add the warm butter in a thin stream while whipping continuously. Continue working until all the butter is added. The mixture should be thick and creamy.

Continued on next page

7. Add the tarragon reduction.

8. Season to taste with salt and pepper. Keep in a warm location in a crock or insulated container until needed, but don't leave too long. This sauce is very unstable during changes in temperature.

FOR THE TEMPURA SOFT-SHELL CRAB:

1. Place oil in large pot. Attach a thermometer to the side of the pan and heat oil to 350 degrees.

2. Clean the soft-shell crabs using kitchen shears. Cut off the face by half an inch. Remove the lungs on both sides by pulling up on each side of the top shell and cutting them out. Remove the skirt on the bottom of the crab. Press the stomach and calcium deposits out of the crab through the opening where the face was removed, **[1-4]**.

3. Place the soft-shell crabs on paper towels and press them dry. Keep refrigerated until ready to use.

4. Line a small bowl with paper towels.

5. Holding the hind legs, dip crabs in Tempura Batter, **[5]**, and carefully add to hot oil. Be sure not to overcrowd the pan. You may need to cook in two batches. Cook for 2 1/2 to 3 minutes, flipping the crabs as needed.

6. Remove crabs from oil, **[6]**, and place in bowl with paper towels to absorb excess oil. Season with fine sea salt.

FOR ASSEMBLY:

1. Place the veal breast on a tray, season with salt and pepper and add 1/4 cup water. Place in the oven to heat through, 8 to 10 minutes. Brush veal sauce over the breast prior to serving.

2. On six serving plates, place equal amounts of asparagus. Lay the veal breast on top of the asparagus and place a tablespoon of sauce on top of the veal. Stand half of a soft-shell crab next to the veal and spoon the béarnaise around the plate. Finish with a few grains of sea salt over the veal breast.

YIELDS 6 SERVINGS

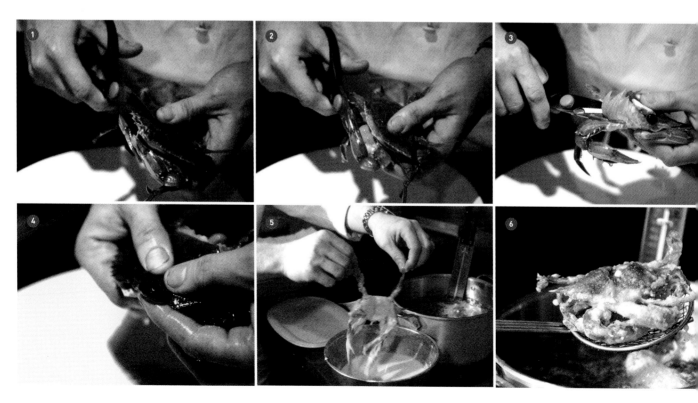

DECONSTRUCTED LAMB T-BONE
WITH ENGLISH PEA RISOTTO

1 lamb saddle, split, boned, rolled, seasoned with
   salt and pepper, and tied*
Canola oil
6 sprigs thyme
6 cloves garlic, crushed
3 tablespoons butter
Extra virgin olive oil
Coarse sea salt

ENGLISH PEA RISOTTO
4 cups water
4 tablespoons olive oil
2 tablespoons minced shallots
2 tablespoons minced garlic
2 cups carniroli or Arborio rice
¼ cup white wine
1 cup English peas, blanched

¼ cup goat cheese (fromage blanc)
Salt
White pepper
2 tablespoons finely chopped mint

The lamb saddle is basically a New York strip and tenderloin. English peas are best in Charleston in the early spring and run for about six weeks. I suggest you buy them unshelled. The pod ensures that the peas will keep their sweetness longer before turning starchy.

1. Preheat oven to 350 degrees.
2. Place a large sauté pan over medium-high heat and add enough canola oil to cover the bottom of the pan by 1/8 inch. Let the oil get hot.
3. Carefully add the lamb to the hot oil and sear for 2 minutes on all sides. Lower the temperature to medium if the pan gets too hot.
4. Place the pan in the oven and cook for 5 minutes.
5. Remove the pan from the oven and add the thyme, garlic and butter and roll the lamb in the pan. Baste the lamb with the melted butter and herbs. Place back in the oven and cook for 3 minutes.
6. Remove the lamb from the pan and place on a tray to rest for 5 minutes.
7. Cut and remove butcher's twine. Slice the lamb into 8 slices per piece.
8. On four serving plates, place an equal amount of English Pea Risotto in a line on the center of the plate. Fan 4 slices of lamb over the risotto. Finish with 1 tablespoon extra virgin olive oil and a sprinkle of coarse sea salt over the lamb.

FOR THE ENGLISH PEA RISOTTO:

1. Place water in a small saucepan and bring to a simmer over medium heat.
2. Place a large saucepan over medium heat and add olive oil, shallots and garlic. Cook for 3 minutes. Shallots and garlic should be translucent.
3. Add the rice and stir with shallots and garlic; cook another 3 minutes. The rice should be golden and smell nutty.
4. Add white wine to the rice and cook for 1 minute, stirring constantly.
5. Slowly add 1/4 cup of the hot water to the rice, stirring constantly from this point out. Continue to add water 1/4 cup at a time every 2 to 3 minutes. After 1 1/2 cups of water has been added, add the blanched peas and goat cheese. Stir in 1/2 cup of water and continue to cook 2 to 3 minutes, while stirring constantly. Add another 1/2 cup of water. Season to taste with salt and pepper. If the risotto has a slight bite to it, add another 1/4 cup water and continue to stir. Risotto should be creamy and firm when done.
6. Stir in chopped mint directly before serving risotto and add remaining water if the risotto is tight.

YIELDS 4 SERVINGS

*see photos on next page

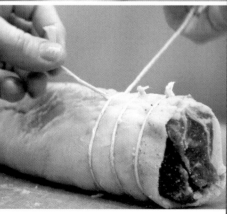

lamb saddle, split, boned, rolled, and tied

GARLIC AND HERB ROASTED RACK OF LAMB
WITH CHÂTEAU POTATOES, HARICOTS VERTS AND BALSAMIC LAMB REDUCTION

2 (8-bone) lamb racks, frenched	2 tablespoons minced garlic	2 tablespoons butter
Salt	3 tablespoons olive oil	1 pound haricots verts, trimmed and blanched
Black pepper	2 tablespoons butter	Salt
1 tablespoon rosemary	1 bulb garlic, cut in half	White pepper
1 tablespoon sage	6 sprigs thyme	Château Potatoes (see p. 173)
1 tablespoon thyme	2 sprigs rosemary	

We serve this hearty dish tableside at Cypress; it makes quite a statement. The photos illustrate the "frenching" butchery technique; if it's too much to do at home, your butcher can "french" the bones on request.

1. Preheat oven to 350 degrees.
2. Wrap the visible lamb bones in aluminum foil. This will keep them bright white when cooked.
3. Season lamb racks with salt and pepper and leave at room temperature for 20 minutes.
4. In a spice grinder, combine the rosemary, sage and thyme. Pulse fine.
5. In a small bowl, mix the garlic, olive oil and finely chopped herbs.
6. Rub the herb mixture evenly over the lamb racks.
7. Place the lamb racks in a roasting pan, bone sides down. Place in the oven for 10 minutes.

8. Pull the pan out and close the oven door. Flip the lamb racks so the meat side is down and add the butter, garlic, thyme and rosemary. Place the pan back in the oven for another 5 minutes and cook. Remove from oven and baste the meat with the fat and juices.
9. Place the lamb racks on a clean tray and rest for 10 minutes.
10. Place a large sauté pan over medium heat and add the butter. When butter is melted, add the haricots verts and cook 2 minutes. Season with salt and pepper to taste and keep warm.
11. Place the lamb racks on a cutting board and cut into 8 double bone chops.
12. On four serving plates, place 5 Chateau Potatoes and an equal amount of haricots verts. Place 2 lamb chops on each plate and finish with lamb reduction around the plate.

YIELDS 4 SERVINGS

BRAISED LAMB SHANKS
WITH ROQUEFORT POLENTA AND ROASTED BEETS

4 lamb shanks
4 tablespoons olive oil
2 tablespoons crushed garlic
2 tablespoons chopped rosemary
Salt
White pepper
½ cup chopped onion
¼ cup chopped leeks

¼ cup chopped carrot
¼ cup chopped celery
1 cup port wine
4 sprigs rosemary
6 cups Veal Stock (see p. 31)
6 cups water
Salt
Pepper
Roasted Beets (see p. 159)

ROQUEFORT POLENTA
2 cups water
¼ cup crumbled Roquefort
½ cup polenta
1 tablespoon salt
1 teaspoon white pepper
4 tablespoons butter

The ultimate comfort food, braised lamb shanks, is well worth the cooking time that this recipe requires. The Roquefort polenta has a distinctive "gamey" goat cheese flavor. It's a perfect complement to the dish and catches the last drops of the delicious sauce.

1. Preheat oven to 350 degrees.
2. In a roasting pan, combine lamb shanks, olive oil, garlic, rosemary, salt and pepper, [1].
3. Place roasting pan in the oven for 30 minutes. Lamb shanks should be a rich brown color, [2]. Remove from oven.
4. Lower temperature to 250 degrees.
5. In a large pot, combine onion, leeks, carrot, celery, port wine, and rosemary, [3]. Cover with cheesecloth and place lamb shanks on top, [4] [5]. Add the stock and water. This should cover lamb shanks by a little more than half.
6. Cover pot with a tight lid or aluminum foil. Place in oven and cook for 6 hours.
7. When lamb shanks are done, remove from oven and allow to cool.
8. When cool, place in refrigerator for one full day.
9. Preheat oven to 300 degrees.
10. Break fat cap off top layer in pan and remove lamb shanks. Keep refrigerated until ready to use.

11. Place pan on the stove over medium-high heat and bring to a simmer. When sauce has returned to a liquid state, strain through a fine sieve into another pan; discard the vegetables.
12. Place pan back over heat and reduce liquid by two-thirds. Skim fat and scum that rises to the surface. Season with salt and pepper to taste. The sauce should be syrupy.
13. Place lamb shanks in a roasting pan and heat for 20 minutes.
14. On four serving plates, place equal amounts of Roasted Beets, 1/2 cup Roquefort Polenta, 1 lamb shank and finish with lamb jus.

ROQUEFORT POLENTA:

1. Place the water in a small saucepan and bring to a boil over high heat.
2. When boiling, add the Roquefort and stir constantly until melted.
3. Add the polenta while stirring, lower the heat to medium and continue to stir until the polenta absorbs the water. Remove from heat, cover with a lid or wrap tightly and let sit for 35 minutes; the polenta will finish cooking by steam.
4. Stir in the salt, pepper and butter and keep warm.

YIELDS 4 SERVINGS

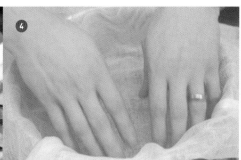

{ A C C O M P A N I M E N T S }

8

BRUSSELS SPROUTS WITH BACON, SHALLOTS AND GARLIC

Water	1 pound Brussels sprouts, cut into ¼ inch slices	2 tablespoons thinly sliced garlic
Salt	4 ounces slab bacon (¼ inch cubes)	3 tablespoons Herb Butter (see p. 26)
	4 tablespoons thinly sliced shallots	

1. Blanch small batches of Brussels sprouts in boiling salt water for 3 minutes and shock in ice water. When cold, drain and pat dry.

2. Place a sauté pan over medium heat and add the bacon. Render the bacon until caramelized. Remove half of the bacon fat and add the shallots and garlic. Caramelize for 3 minutes.

3. Add the Brussels sprouts and cook for 2 minutes.

4. Remove the pan from heat and add the Herb Butter and mix until melted and incorporated. The butter should provide a creamy coat to the Brussels sprouts.

5. Serve immediately.

YIELDS 4 SERVINGS

SUCCOTASH FRICASSEE

6 cups water	¼ cup crowder peas (black-eyed peas are a good substitute)	¼ cup minced chives
3 tablespoons kosher salt	½ cup Hominy (see p. 210)	2 tablespoons kosher salt
¼ cup butter beans	2 tablespoons butter	1 teaspoon white pepper

1. In a heavy-bottom saucepan, combine water, salt, butter beans and crowder peas.

2. Bring to a low simmer and cook for 25 minutes. Skim off any scum that rises to the surface.

3. The beans should have a firm skin with a soft and creamy inside. Remove from heat and shock the beans in an ice bath.

4. Mix the beans and the Hominy together.

5. With a sauté pan over medium-high heat, add the butter until melted. Add the hominy mixture and cook until hot. Add the chives, salt and pepper.

6. Incorporate evenly, taste and adjust seasoning if needed; keep warm.

YIELDS 4 SERVINGS

CARAMELIZED FENNEL

1 large bulb fennel, trimmed to bulb only (save a few fronds for garnish) 1 large onion, peeled and cut in half	¼ cup extra virgin olive oil ½ tablespoon salt ½ teaspoon white pepper	1/2 teaspoon lemon zest 3 tablespoons Lemon Butter (see p. 25)

1. Cut the fennel in half and remove the core. Slice the fennel into 1/4-inch slices.
2. Remove the core of the onion and discard. Cut the rest of the onion the same thickness as the fennel.
3. Place a large pan over medium-high heat. When hot, add the olive oil, fennel and onion and cook for 5 minutes. Lower the temperature to medium and cook another 5 minutes. The onions and fennel should be soft and caramelized.

4. Season with salt, pepper, and lemon zest; incorporate evenly.
5. Remove from heat and place in a warm location. Reheat before serving if needed.
6. Stir in the Lemon Butter before serving.

YIELDS 4 SERVINGS

CRUSHED RED POTATOES

1½ pounds red bliss potatoes, washed well and cut in quarters 3 tablespoons salt	Water ¼ cup butter, cut into cubes 2 tablespoons salt	1 teaspoon white pepper 2 tablespoons finely chopped chives

This recipe jazzes up traditional red potatoes for a great side dish with meats and poultry.

1. In a small pot, combine the potatoes and salt and completely cover with cold water. Place over medium heat and cook 15 minutes. Potatoes should be fork tender.

2. Transfer the potatoes to a colander and drain.
3. Place the potatoes back into the pot and crush with a fork. Stir in butter, salt, pepper and chives. Adjust seasonings, if needed.
4. Keep the potatoes in a warm area. If you have a lid use it, or wrap tightly with food film.

YIELDS 4 SERVINGS

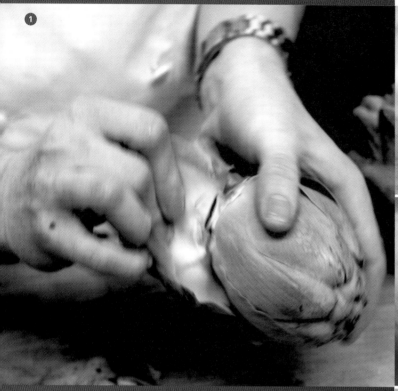

artichokes

3 lemons, juiced
4 cups water
4 medium artichokes
¼ cup extra virgin olive oil
¼ cup diced onion
¼ cup diced carrots
1 bouquet garni (basil, thyme, and tarragon)
½ cup white wine
2 tablespoons salt
½ teaspoon white pepper

1. In a mixing bowl, combine lemon juice and water.
2. Peel away the outer leaves of the artichokes. [1] Lay the
artichokes on a cutting board, and cut the top of the artichoke
where the leaves start to change from yellow to green, about 1
inch from the base. [2] Peel the stems and trim away the
firm green skin. [3] [4] Place the artichokes in the lemon
water. [5]

3. In a saucepan combine the olive oil, onion, and carrots. Place over medium heat and sweat for 4 minutes.

4. Add the artichokes and lemon water to the saucepan along with bouquet garni, white wine, salt and pepper.

5. Bring to a low simmer and cook for 35 minutes. Artichokes should be fork tender.

6. Remove from heat and allow to cool in the liquid. Remove the bouquet garni. If you are using the artichoke immediately, proceed; if not, place in the refrigerator.

7. Slice the artichokes in half and remove the thistle in the center with a spoon. [6] [7]. Place the artichokes back in the liquid with onions and carrots.

8. To reheat, place the artichokes, carrots and onion back into a saucepan and place over medium heat. This will take about 5 minutes. Artichokes should be warm through. [8] Season the liquid with salt and white pepper if needed.

YIELDS 4 SERVINGS

POTATO GRATIN

½ cup heavy cream
2 eggs

½ cup grated Parmesan cheese
1½ tablespoons salt
1 teaspoon white pepper

½ teaspoon grated nutmeg
4 large russet potatoes, peeled
¼ cup cornmeal

These can also be made in a casserole pan.

1. Preheat oven to 300 degrees.
2. In a mixing bowl, combine the heavy cream, eggs, Parmesan, salt, pepper and nutmeg, using a whisk to incorporate evenly.
3. Cut the ends off of the potatoes and slice very thin on a Japanese mandoline. Add the sliced potatoes to the cream mixture and coat all the slices.
4. Using pan spray, coat a cupcake pan evenly and dust the molds with the cornmeal. Add the sliced potatoes to the molds by stacking the slices one on top of the other. Mix remaining liquid and add to the molds. You may not need all the liquid.
5. Wrap the pan with aluminum foil and cook for 45 minutes. Remove the foil and cook for 25 minutes to brown the tops. Potatoes should be tender when pierced with a fork.
6. Remove from oven and cool for 10 minutes. Run a knife around the molds, place a tray on top of the potatoes and flip the pan over to pop the potatoes out. To serve, flip the gratins back over, showing the golden crust.

YIELDS 4 SERVINGS

GRUYÈRE POTATO FONDUE

3 pounds Yukon gold potatoes, peeled and cut into
   ½-inch thick rounds

2 tablespoons salt
1½ cups heavy cream
½ cup grated gruyère cheese

½ cup butter, cut into cubes
1½ tablespoons salt
1½ teaspoons white pepper

1. In a large pot, add potatoes and salt and cover with water.
2. Place over medium heat and cook for 25 minutes. Potatoes should split when pierced with a fork.
3. Transfer the potatoes to a colander and drain.
4. Place a food mill attached with the smallest screen over the pot you cooked the potatoes in. Work the hot potatoes through the food mill.
5. Add the heavy cream and gruyère cheese to the potatoes and fold in evenly. The cheese will get stringy as it melts.
6. Stir in the butter cubes until melted. The potatoes should have a velvety consistency.
7. Season with the salt and pepper and incorporate evenly. Adjust seasoning if needed.
8. Keep the potatoes in a warm area. If you have a lid, use it or wrap tightly with food film.

YIELDS 4 SERVINGS

goat cheese grits

2 cups water
½ cup stone-ground white grits
1½ tablespoons salt
2 teaspoons white pepper
½ cup goat cheese
1½ teaspoons lemon zest

1. Place water in a saucepan and bring to a boil.
2. Add the grits to the boiling water and stir with a small whisk. Reduce the temperature to medium and continue stirring for 5 minutes until the grits absorb the water, **[1] [2] [3] [4]**.
3. Remove from heat and cover with a lid or wrap tightly with food film, **[5]**. Set in a warm area for 35 minutes; the grits will finish cooking by steam.
4. Add the salt, pepper, goat cheese and lemon zest; incorporate evenly, **[6] [7]**. Cover tightly and keep warm.

YIELDS 4 SERVINGS

making hominy

At Cypress we have a wood burning grill and a wood smoker, both of which produce ashes. We use the ashes to create lye, which is the alkaline used in making hominy. Lye softens the skin and allows it to be removed from the corn. This process is what makes hominy different from grits.

It is essential that nonreactive cookware be used to prepare hominy. The pots must be stainless steel or enamel-coated cast iron. The utensils must be either wood or stainless steel. The measuring cups should be glass. You should wear

gloves. At this strength, the lye will not burn your skin, but it will cause discomfort if it comes in contact with bare skin. If you do get it on your skin, rinse with white vinegar to stop the burn.

½ gallon of ash (from a hardwood fire)
1½ quarts water
1 pound dried hominy corn

Combine the water and ash in a large glass container. The mixture should be thick and sludgy. Place a lid on the mixture and let this sit for at least a day. All of the soot will settle to the bottom and can be seen through the glass. Strain the clear liquid on top through a chinois. This will eliminate big pieces, but there still may be some ash in the water.

Add this water to the dried yellow hominy corn. The kernels will gradually turn from yellow-orange to grayish black, which indicates that the process is working. Cover and put in a cool place, but do not refrigerate. Let sit for at least a day. Three days yields a superior finished product.

After the corn has soaked for the elapsed time, add lye and corn to a large nonreactive pot. Cook over medium-low heat. Always keep at a simmer or no hotter than 180 degrees. There should never be any bubbles. Stir every half hour. After about 3 hours, start stirring the kernels every 5 minutes. As the mixture gets thick and sludgy, the skin starts to melt off of the kernels.

When all of the hulls seem to be off, rinse the kernels. Rinse well because it's important to get the hulls off. Rinse the pot well. Return the kernels to the pot and add enough water to cover by 1/2 inch. They will start to absorb fresh water. Cook over low heat until the kernels begin to soften. They should feel almost like firm or raw field peas. Rinse the corn kernels again.

Return the kernels to the pot and add enough water to cover by 1/2-inch. The kernels should almost be fully cooked. Continue to cook the kernels over low heat for about 30 minutes. Taste one every few minutes. When the kernels are done, they should have a slightly firm center. Drain, rinse, and shock the kernels in iced water; drain again. If you see any little hulls, rub the kernel in your hands to break off every last bit of skin. You can also do this between every rinsing process.

If not used within a couple of days, the hominy can be frozen.

YIELDS 4 CUPS

9

{ D E S S E R T S }

the recipes

Chocolate Peanut Butter Caramel Cake

Green Tea Crème Brûlée

Key Lime White Chocolate Cheesecake

Fruit and Cheese

Grand Marnier Soufflé

Warm Molten Chocolate Cake

Autumn-Spiced Dessert Spring Rolls

As pastry chef at Cypress, Kelly Wilson (above) wraps up our meals, finishing them with just the right amount of sweetness that reminds you once again why eating is such a pleasure. Kelly focuses on using flavors familiar to our dinners, and strives to provide desserts with recognizable and beloved components. Chocolate, peanut butter, orange, caramel, apple, vanilla, peach, hazelnut, and strawberry are simply a few of the "common" flavors on which she bases her creations.

Crème brûlée, soufflés, cheesecakes, tarts, pies, cakes, and tortes are some of the products Kelly uses to present these flavors. The key, however, lies in elevating these common flavors and standard products into desserts which are uncommon and nonstandard, delicious, and potentially addictive. Quality of ingredients and the knowledge of how to manipulate, combine, and reshape them is what is required to create truly amazing tasting and great-looking desserts.

CHOCOLATE PEANUT BUTTER CARAMEL CAKE

JOANN'S CHOCOLATE-BUTTERMILK CAKE
4 cups all-purpose flour
12 tablespoons cocoa powder
4 cups granulated sugar
1 pound unsalted butter, melted
2 cups water
1 cup buttermilk

4 large eggs
2 teaspoons vanilla extract
2 teaspoons baking soda

PEANUT BUTTER CARAMEL MASCARPONE FILLING
1 cup granulated sugar
¼ cup light corn syrup

½ cup water
1 cup heavy cream
2 tablespoons unsalted butter
¾ cup creamy peanut butter
½ vanilla bean pod, split and scraped
   (or 2 teaspoons vanilla extract)

I love this cake. In the five years we have worked together, it's the one dessert that I have made. Kelly's version is an adaptation of my recipe (known as Craig's Better Than Sex Cake), which is an interpretation of my mom's famous Chocolate Astronaut Cake.

All three variations of this cake contain three core elements: chocolate cake, caramel, and peanut butter. When Kelly developed this recipe for my wedding cake, she kept my mother's excellent cake recipe, titled "Joann's Chocolate Buttermilk-Cake" below, played with the caramel and peanut butter filling, and came up with Chocolate Peanut Butter Layer Cake.

FOR JOANN'S CHOCOLATE-BUTTERMILK CAKE:

1. Preheat oven to 350 degrees.
2. Spray three 9-inch-round cake pans with pan spray. Line the bottoms of the pans with parchment (or wax) paper. Spray the pans again. This assures the cakes will release cleanly and easily after cooling.
3. In a large bowl, sift together the flour and cocoa powder. Add the granulated sugar and whisk to combine.
4. In a separate bowl, combine hot melted butter and water.
5. In another bowl, whisk together buttermilk, eggs, and vanilla extract.
6. Whisk the butter mixture into the flour mixture.
7. Add the egg mixture next. Whisk until well combined.
8. Sift the baking soda over the batter. Stir until fully incorporated.

9. Divide the batter between the prepared pans.
10. Bake for 10 minutes in the oven, rotate the pans (to ensure even baking), and bake for another 10 minutes. Check the cakes for doneness; if a skewer inserted in the center of the cake comes out with wet batter clinging to it, bake for an additional 5 minutes and check again. When the skewer comes out clean—no wet batter, but a few moist crumbs are acceptable—then remove cakes from the oven.
11. Cool the cakes for 15 minutes in the pans. Remove from the pans and cool completely on cooling racks.

YIELDS 3 (9-INCH-ROUND) CAKE LAYERS

FOR THE PEANUT BUTTER CARAMEL MASCARPONE FILLING:

1. Combine the sugar, corn syrup, and water in a nonreactive, heavy-bottomed pot with high sides. Stir until all the sugar is moist. Make sure there are no sugar crystals clinging to the sides of the pot. Any errant crystals can "infect" the caramel, causing the sugar to recrystallize and result in a gritty texture. Wash the sides of the pot down with a pastry brush dipped in water to remove the crystals.
2. Place the pot over high heat and bring to a boil. As the water evaporates, the syrup becomes very thick. Within 10 or 15 minutes, the syrup will begin to turn an amber color around the edge of the pot. Gently swirl the pot to redistribute the heat and ensure that the sugar does not overcook in one spot while not cooking long enough in another. As the caramel continues to cook, it will darken.

Continued on next page

GLAZING GANACHE

9 ounces bittersweet chocolate, finely chopped

3 tablespoons unsalted butter, cubed

¾ cup heavy cream

2 tablespoons light corn syrup

PEANUT-COCOA NIB BRITTLE

1 cup granulated sugar

2 tablespoons light corn syrup

⅓ cup water

1 tablespoon Frangelico

½ teaspoon baking soda

⅔ cup roasted peanuts

¼ cup cocoa nibs

3. When the caramel reaches a dark amber (roughly 330 degrees), it's time to "shock" it. To do this, remove the pot from the heat and carefully add the cream. The caramel will sputter. Once the initial reaction is complete, begin to whisk the caramel. There may be hardened clumps of caramel in the mixture; this is normal. Simply return the pot to medium-high heat and stir gently.

4. Once the caramel smoothes out, add the butter, peanut butter, vanilla and salt. Stir until smooth.

5. Remove the caramel from the heat and strain through a chinois or other fine strainer into a metal container.

6. Place the metal container in an ice bath and stir intermittently. Replace ice as necessary. Once the caramel is completely cooled (40–50 degrees is the best temperature range), scrape it into the bowl of a mixer. Add cold mascarpone to the bowl and beat using the paddle attachment until combined and stiff. Scrape the bottom of the mixer bowl to be sure that all of the cheese is incorporated into the caramel. Remove the peanut butter caramel cream from the bowl and store in the refrigerator until ready to use.

ASSEMBLING THE CHOCOLATE PEANUT BUTTER LAYER CAKE

1. Place each of the cooled cake layers on a cutting board. Using a large serrated bread knife, trim each layer so that the top is flat (save the scraps for snacking). Cover the first layer with one-third of the Peanut Butter Caramel Mascarpone Filling.

Make sure the filling is flat. Top this with cake layer number two. Cover with one-third of the caramel cream. Finally, top it all off with the third cake layer. Spread the remaining filling over the outside of the cake—the smoother, the better. The idea is to give the cake what is called a crumb coating. Also, the ganache coating that finishes the cake will cling better to the cream than to naked cake.

2. Once the cake is covered, freeze it for at least 4 hours, preferably overnight. Once frozen, the cake will be ready for its ganache coating.

FOR THE GLAZING GANACHE:

Ganache at its simplest is an emulsion of heavy cream and chocolate. It is a basis for everything from truffles to cake coatings to mousses. The texture of ganache is manipulated by varying the ratio of cream to chocolate in the recipe. The quality of the ganache rests on the quality of the chocolate. I recommend European chocolates such as Callebaut, Valrhona, and Lindt. Avoid chocolate chips because emulsifiers and stabilizers have been added.

1. Combine the chocolate and butter in a bowl.

2. Combine the cream and corn syrup in a small pot. Over a medium flame, heat the cream and corn syrup until it steams and bubbles begin to pop up around the edge of the pot.

3. Remove the pot from the heat and pour the warm liquid over the chocolate and butter. Give the bowl a couple of gentle shakes to settle the chocolate down into the cream. Let the mixture rest for a minute or two.

4. Stir carefully until all the chocolate and butter have melted and the ganache is smooth and shiny.

GLAZING THE CHOCOLATE PEANUT BUTTER LAYER CAKE:

1.   Remove the cake from the freezer and place it on a wire cooling rack. Place the rack and cake over a sheet pan covered with a sheet of parchment paper.

2.   With a large, offset, cake decorator's spatula handy, pour the ganache over the top of the frozen cake. I find it best to pour in a circular pattern about halfway between the edge and the center of the cake. Use the spatula to smooth the ganache so that it completely covers the cake and runs over the edges. Run the spatula over the sides of the cake, redistributing the ganache to cover the entire sides of the cake. Give the wire rack a couple of good taps to settle everything. Remove the cake from the rack, arrange it on a serving plate, and place it in the refrigerator to quickly set the ganache.

3.   After the ganache is set, slice the cake using a chef's knife. (Hot water is the key to an artfully sliced serving of cake. Fill a large container with hot water. Place the knife, tip down, in the water. When ready to slice, remove the knife, dry it carefully, and cut. Dip the knife in the hot water and dry it between each slice.)

FOR THE PEANUT-COCOA NIB BRITTLE:

This brittle serves as an apt garnish for the Chocolate Peanut Butter Caramel Cake. It has the main elements of our cake: peanuts allude to the peanut butter in the filling, cocoa nibs represent the chocolate, and the caramel base of the brittle echoes the caramel in the filling. Here we make a caramel following the same method as the Peanut Butter Caramel filling. Refer to that recipe for tips on making caramel.

1.   Combine the sugar, corn syrup, and water in a small saucepan. Be sure the sugar is completely hydrated. Wash down the sides of the pot if there are any sugar crystals lingering.

2.   Bring to a boil over high heat without disturbing the pot. In 3 to 5 minutes, the sugar will begin to caramelize. Swirl the syrup in the pot to redistribute the heat. When the syrup is light amber throughout, remove from the heat and add the Frangelico and baking soda. (This step results in tiny air bubbles in the brittle.) Stir carefully as the baking soda reacts with the heat. Return to medium heat, add the peanuts and cocoa nibs, and stir gently to coat.

3.   Pour the brittle onto a nonstick baking mat. Let the brittle stand for approximately 2 minutes. It should cool slightly, but remain warm. Stretch the mixture with your fingers to make a thin, thin sheet of brittle. Allow to cool completely. Break into pieces and store at room temperature in an airtight container until needed.

YIELDS ROUGHLY 16 PIECES

GREEN TEA CRÈME BRÛLÉE

1 cup whole milk
½ cup turbinado sugar, divided
⅛ cup gunpowder green tea leaves
1 teaspoon matcha green tea powder
Pinch of ground allspice
Zest of half a lime

1 teaspoon freshly grated ginger
7 large egg yolks
2½ cups heavy cream
Granulated sugar, as needed
Crystallized ginger

CARAMELIZED RICE KRISPIES
¼ cup granulated sugar
3 tablespoons corn syrup
Water
4 tablespoons butter, cubed
2 cups Rice Krispies

This custard hits your taste buds running. After cracking into the sugary shell, your first bite starts off with the unmistakable tang of ginger, follows with the sweetness of the sugar, and finishes with the tannic flavor of the teas. Kelly uses both types of tea in this brûlée in order to intensify the subtleness of the green tea.

1. Combine milk, half the sugar, gunpowder green tea leaves, matcha green tea powder, allspice, lime zest, and ginger in a medium saucepan. Bring to a boil. Cover and remove from heat. Allow the mixture to steep for 30 minutes.
2. Meanwhile, in a separate bowl, whisk together yolks and remaining sugar.
3. Remove the cover and return the steeped milk and tea mixture to a boil. Slowly whisk the hot milk mixture into the yolks.
4. Strain the mixture through a fine chinois. Add the cream. Stir and chill in an ice bath. For best results, allow the crème brûlée base to rest overnight.
5. Arrange four 8-ounce ramekins on a level sheet pan with at least a 3/4-inch lip. Fill the dishes with the chilled brûlée base. Carefully place the pan in a 300-degree oven. Fill the sheetpan with hot water. Bake the custards for 30 to 40 minutes or until the center of each is almost set.

6. Remove ramekins from the oven and chill completely.
7. When ready to serve, spread an even layer of granulated sugar on the surface of each crème brûlée. Caramelize the sugar with a propane torch.
8. Garnish with crystallized ginger and Caramelized Rice Krispies. Serve immediately.

FOR THE CARAMELIZED RICE KRISPIES:

1. Combine the sugar, corn syrup, and water in a medium saucepan. Be sure the sugar is completely hydrated. Wash down the sides of the pot if there are any sugar crystals lingering.
2. Bring to a boil over high heat without disturbing the pot. In 3 to 5 minutes, the sugar will begin to caramelize. Swirl the syrup in the pot to redistribute the heat.
3. When the syrup is light amber throughout, stir the butter into the caramel until smooth.
4. Stir in the Rice Krispies while the pot is over medium heat. Stir until the cereal is evenly coated.
5. Pour onto a Silpat and smooth with a metal spatula. Cool and break into chunks.
6. Store in an airtight container.

YIELDS 4 (8-OUNCE) CRÈME BRÛLÉES

KEY LIME WHITE CHOCOLATE CHEESECAKE

1½ pounds cream cheese, room temperature
½ cup sugar
Pinch of nutmeg
1 teaspoon vanilla extract
3 whole large eggs, room temperature
2 egg yolks, room temperature
1 pound quality white chocolate, finely chopped
6 ounces key lime juice, room temperature
2 tablespoons Meyer's Dark Rum

HOMEMADE GRAHAM CRACKERS
2½ cups all-purpose flour
½ cup whole wheat flour
¼ cup light brown sugar
1 teaspoon baking soda
½ teaspoon ground cinnamon
¾ teaspoon salt
6 tablespoons butter, soft
½ cup honey

½ teaspoon vanilla extract
⅓ cup cold water

GINGERED BLUEBERRY COMPOTE
3 cups fresh blueberries
⅓ cup sugar
1 (3-inch) piece gingerroot, peeled and sliced
   thinly
Juice of 1 lime

This outstanding cheesecake is a continual hit among our diners. It features the elements of the traditional key lime pie morphed into a cheesecake, one of the most popular of all desserts in America.

1.   Preheat oven to 325 degrees.
2.   Using an electric mixer, cream together cream cheese, sugar, nutmeg and vanilla extract.
3.   Add the eggs and yolks individually to the cream cheese mixture. Scrape the bowl often.
4.   Melt the white chocolate by placing it in a microwave-safe container and microwaving in 30-second increments at half power, stirring between each cooking interval. Continue cooking and stirring until chocolate is smooth.
5.   Fold melted chocolate into the cream cheese base until completely incorporated.
6.   Combine key lime juice and rum and fold into the batter.
7.   Using pan spray, grease twelve 4-ounce aluminum tins or a muffin pan with 12 cups. Divide the batter amongst the tins or cups, filling each to within 1/4 inch of the top.
8.   Place tins or muffin pan in a sheet pan with at least a 3/4-inch lip. Put the pan of cheesecakes in the oven and carefully fill the sheet pan to the top with hot water. Bake for 20 minutes and check for doneness. Continue baking as needed. The center of each cheesecake should be set.
9.   Remove the cheesecakes from the oven and cool for 1 hour on a wire rack. For best results, chill overnight before unmolding.

FOR THE HOMEMADE GRAHAM CRACKERS:
1.   Combine flours, sugar, baking soda, cinnamon and salt in an electric mixing bowl. Using the paddle attachment, mix on low for 30 seconds.
2.   Add the remaining ingredients and mix until just smooth.
3.   Wrap and chill the dough, preferably overnight.
4.   Roll the dough out to about 1/8 inch thick. Cut the dough with a round cookie cutter that is roughly the size of the base of the individual cheesecakes. (The top of the cheesecake when it is in the forms is actually going to be the bottom when the dessert is presented.)
5.   Arrange the dough circles on a parchment-lined baking sheet and bake at 325 degrees for approximately 8 minutes. The crackers should be golden in color and soft in texture.
6.   Store at room temperature in an airtight container until needed.

FOR THE GINGERED BLUEBERRY COMPOTE:
1.   Combine all ingredients in a medium pot.
2.   Stir over medium heat until sugar dissolves and berries release juice.
3.   Simmer and cook until about half of the berries have burst, 3 to 4 minutes.
4.   Chill and strain before using, reserving the syrup for the Magenta Lime Chips. Also, be sure to remove the ginger slices from the compote before serving.

Continued on next page

MAGENTA LIME CHIPS

2 limes

Gingered blueberry syrup (reserved from the making of Gingered Blueberry Compote)

WHITE CHOCOLATE-GRAHAM CRACKER MOONS

1 pound white chocolate, finely chopped

¼ cup graham cracker crumbs

WHITE CHOCOLATE SAUCE

½ cup sugar

¼ cup corn syrup

¾ cup water

10 ounces white chocolate, finely chopped

FOR THE MAGENTA LIME CHIPS

1. Using an electric slicer or a Japanese mandoline, cut each lime into slices approximately 1/16 inch thick.
2. Soak the lime slices, excluding the smaller end pieces, overnight in the blueberry syrup.
3. Drain the syrup and place the slices in a single layer—not allowing them to touch—on a nonstick baking mat. Bake in a 200-degree oven for at least 2 hours, or until dry and crisp when cool.
4. Store in an airtight container.

FOR THE WHITE CHOCOLATE-GRAHAM CRACKER MOONS

1. Melt the white chocolate by placing it in a microwave-safe container and microwaving in 30-second increments at half power, stirring between each cooking interval. Continue cooking and stirring until chocolate is smooth.
2. Stir graham cracker crumbs into the melted chocolate.
3. Pour the mixture onto a sheet pan lined with a Silpat and spread with a metal offset spatula until smooth.
4. Place the pan in the refrigerator until the chocolate is just barely set.
5. Using the same round cutter from slicing the graham crackers, cut out half moons. Do this by stamping out one circle, removing the cutter from the chocolate while leaving the chocolate circle in place, then moving to the right about half an inch and cutting another circle. Repeat for more moons.
6. Return the pan to the refrigerator and cool until the chocolate is completely set. Remove from the nonstick mat and store at room temperature until needed.

FOR THE WHITE CHOCOLATE SAUCE

1. Combine sugar, corn syrup and water and bring to a boil. Remove from heat and add white chocolate to the pot. Allow the mixture to stand for 2 minutes.
2. Whisk until smooth and then strain and chill.
3. To thin: add more warm water.
4. To thicken: add melted white chocolate.

ASSEMBLING THE CHEESECAKES

1. Unmold the cheesecakes and place each on a graham cracker.
2. Place a layer of blueberry compote approximately the same size as the graham cracker on a plate. Top with a graham-bottomed cheesecake.
3. Insert a Magenta Lime Chip and a White Chocolate-Graham Cracker Moon into the top of the cake.
4. Using a squeeze bottle, decorate the plate with white chocolate sauce.
5. Sprinkle some lime zest over the entire plate.
6. Serve.

YIELDS 12 (4-OUNCE) CHEESECAKES

CHEF DEIHL'S NOTE: Here are the four keys to cheesecake success: First, have all of the ingredients at room temperature. In the case of cheesecakes, the ingredients mix best at the same, warm temperature.

Second, scrape the mixing bowl often. Don't be afraid to get down in that mixing bowl and ferret out every lump of cream cheese. Fewer lumps result in less chance of overmixing because the batter becomes smoother more quickly. That leads to tip three: overmixing a cheesecake leads to the incorporation of too much air into the batter. When that extra air heats in the oven, steam is trapped, and the cake rises (this is termed "physical leavening"). While this is necessary in a soufflé, it is death to a cheesecake. When the "risen" cheesecake cools, the hot air in it cools and the entire cake shrinks. This results in cracking, which ruins the presentation.

Finally, a water bath is crucial in producing that just right cheesecake. This entails surrounding the pan of cheesecake batter with a warm water bath while it bakes. The water insulates the cheesecake and protects against dramatic heat fluctuations.

FRUIT AND CHEESE

HONEYED GOAT CHEESE

3 cups goat cheese, preferably locally produced and organic

½ cup mascarpone cheese

1 tablespoon, plus 1 teaspoon artisanal honey

A pinch or two of salt (depends on the salinity of the goat cheese)

HONEY WHEAT BRIOCHE

2½ teaspoons active dry yeast

½ cup Guinness stout, room temperature

¼ cup granulated sugar

¼ cup bread flour

2½ cups bread flour

½ cup whole wheat flour

1½ teaspoons salt

5 large eggs, lightly beaten

⅓ cup honey

½ pound butter, room temperature, cut in 16 cubes

ASSEMBLING THE FRUIT AND CHEESE PLATE

Strawberries

Blackberries

Raspberries

Grapes

Pears, sliced

Apples, sliced

Toasted pine nuts

Artisanal honey

The perfect ending to a meal is often the simplest. In this variation of the standard fruit and cheese plate, Kelly uses artisanal products that showcase the flavors of South Carolina. Goat cheese from Split Creek Farm in Anderson and cotton blossom honey from Black Creek Apiaries in her hometown of Hartsville combine with fresh fruit to provide a fitting conclusion to any dinner.

FOR THE HONEYED GOAT CHEESE:

1. Combine all the ingredients in the bowl of an electric mixer. Using the paddle attachment, beat until the ingredients are smooth and well combined.
2. Refrigerate until needed.

FOR THE HONEY WHEAT BRIOCHE:

1. Preheat oven to 400 degrees.
2. In a bowl, whisk together the yeast, Guinness, sugar, and 1/2 cup bread flour. Cover tightly and set in a warm place to proof for 30 to 45 minutes.
3. Using a dough hook, mix 2 1/2 cups bread flour, whole wheat flour, and salt on low speed until combined.
4. Add the yeast mixture, eggs, and honey to the dry ingredients. Mix on low speed for 2 minutes. Turn up to medium and mix for 5 minutes.
5. While mixing on medium speed, add butter one cube at a time. Knead 5 more minutes at medium speed.
6. Remove the dough to an oiled bowl. Wrap and allow to rise at room temperature for 2 hours. Punch down, rewrap, and place in a refrigerator overnight.

7. Remove the dough from the refrigerator, punch it down, and divide it into 8 equal pieces for mini loaves.
8. Flatten out each piece of dough then roll it up like a jellyroll; pinch to seal. Place the dough in greased miniature loaf pans.
9. Wrap pans in loose, greased wrap and allow the bread to rise at room temperature for 2 hours. Press your finger gently into the top of one of the loaves to test if the bread has proofed sufficiently. If the indentation made by your finger remains, the dough needs to proof longer.
10. Bake loaves for 20 minutes. The bread is ready when the internal temperature measures 190 degrees and the loaves sound hollow when tapped.
11. Remove bread from the oven, allow to cool for 5 minutes, then remove from pans. Place the bread on a wire rack to cool.
12. Once completely cool, cut half of the loaves into 1/4-inch-thick slices (wrap the remaining loaves well and freeze for later). Toast the slices in a 325-degree oven until crisp and golden.

YIELDS 8 MINI LOAVES

TO ASSEMBLE THE FRUIT AND CHEESE PLATE:

1. Top each slice of brioche toast with a generous scoop of the honeyed goat cheese.
2. Arrange the topped toast on a platter with the fruit. Sprinkle toasted pine nuts over the plate.
3. Drizzle with more honey.

GRAND MARNIER SOUFFLÉ

Unsalted butter, melted

Granulated sugar

Zest of half an orange

1 cup orange juice, fresh squeezed

½ vanilla bean, split and scraped

½ cup granulated sugar, divided in half

¼ cup all-purpose flour

1 teaspoon cornstarch

3 large egg yolks

6 tablespoons Grand Marnier

4 tablespoons orange juice, fresh squeezed

ASSEMBLING THE SOUFFLÉS

2 cups egg whites

2 tablespoons sugar

GRAND MARNIER CRÈME ANGLAISE

½ cup whole milk

½ cup heavy cream

1 teaspoon vanilla extract

Zest of half an orange

3 tablespoons granulated sugar, divided

6 egg yolks

3 tablespoons Grand Marnier

Soufflés are a major part of the Cypress dessert arsenal. A mainstay of the dessert menu is the Grand Marnier Soufflé served with Grand Marnier Crème Anglaise. Classic in its flavor and presentation—the soufflé cap is pierced tableside and the crème anglaise is poured into its heart—it is easily duplicated at home.

FOR THE SOUFFLÉ BASE:

1. Prepare eight ramekins by brushing the insides with a layer of melted butter.

2. Fill the buttered ramekins with granulated sugar and rotate each one so that the sugar evenly coats the interiors of the dishes. Empty any excess sugar.

3. Combine zest, 1 cup orange juice, vanilla bean pod and seeds, and half the sugar in a nonreactive pot. Bring to a boil.

4. Sift together flour and cornstarch. In a separate bowl, whisk the remaining sugar, then the flour and cornstarch with the yolks.

5. While constantly stirring, slowly pour the hot mixture into the yolk mixture.

6. Return all of the mixture to the pot.

7. Cook over medium heat, whisking constantly.

8. After the mixture becomes thick and boils for approximately 30 seconds, remove from the heat and transfer to a tabletop mixer bowl. Using the paddle attachment, beat the soufflé base on low speed until the bowl no longer feels warm.

9. Turn off the mixer and scrape the bowl with a spatula. Return to low speed and add the Grand Marnier and 4 tablespoons orange juice slowly, scraping the bowl at least once during mixing. If you are planning to make the soufflés immediately, scrape the base into a large mixing bowl. If you are preparing the base for later use, store well-wrapped in the refrigerator.

TO ASSEMBLE THE SOUFFLÉS:

1. Preheat oven to 400 degrees.

2. In a grease-free and completely dry electric mixer bowl, whip the whites and sugar until stiff peaks form, [1].

3. Using a rubber spatula, fold a third of this meringue into the prepared soufflé base, [2]. You do not want to stir or whip the base. The goal here is to keep as much of the air as possible that you incorporated in the meringue in the finished soufflé. Carefully fold the remaining meringue into the lightened base, [3]. If you fold too far, the result is a soupy batter that will not rise.

4. Divide the batter amongst the prepared ramekins, [4].

Continued on next page

5. Pinching the lip of the dish between your thumb and index finger, clean the edge of each ramekin.

6. Bake for approximately 8 to 10 minutes, or until the tops of the soufflés are golden.

7. Remove from the oven—carefully!—and serve immediately, since all soufflés are destined to fall.

FOR THE GRAND MARNIER CRÈME ANGLAISE:

Another classic, crème anglaise offers a creamy decadence to our soufflé. Kelly chose to make a sauce that reinforces the flavors of the Grand Marnier, the orange and the vanilla in the soufflé. (Cypress Chocolate Sauce also works well with the soufflé if you are looking for a chocolatey twist on this standard.)

1. Combine milk, cream, vanilla extract, orange zest and half of the sugar in a small, nonreactive saucepan. Bring to a boil.

2. In a bowl, whisk together remaining sugar and yolks.

3. Slowly pour the hot liquid into the yolks while whisking constantly.

4. Return all the liquid to the pan and cook over low heat, stirring constantly. The sauce will begin to thicken slightly. It is done when the temperature reaches approximately 180 degrees.

5. When done, immediately remove from the heat and strain through a chinois. Cool the mixture in an ice bath.

6. Stir in the Grand Marnier. Store under refrigeration. The anglaise can be used for a maximum of 4 days.

YIELDS 4 SERVINGS

CHEF DEIHL'S NOTE. *Demystifying the soufflé is the goal here. Soufflés are going to fall. It is their nature. That should mitigate some the of novice soufflé maker's trepidation. Careful attention to the details of folding will guarantee success. Just be sure to get the finished product to the table as soon as possible for the maximum effect.*

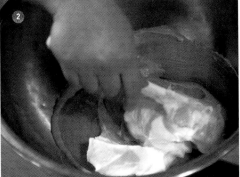

WARM MOLTEN CHOCOLATE CAKE

⅛ cup cocoa powder
⅛ cup all-purpose flour
Cooking spray
11 tablespoons unsalted butter, cubed
5 ounces dark chocolate, finely chopped
3 yolks
3 whole eggs

1 cup powdered sugar
½ cup all-purpose flour

CHOCOLATE SAUCE
1 cup granulated sugar
2 tablespoons light corn syrup
Water

1 cup heavy cream
2 tablespoons butter, cubed
¼ cup cocoa powder
Pinch salt
1 tablespoon vanilla extract
½ cup Vanilla Bean Simple Syrup

The molten chocolate cake is Cypress's most requested dessert. Serve this cake with a generous scoop of high quality vanilla bean ice cream and the plates will come back to the kitchen practically licked clean.

At the restaurant, we use 4-ounce aluminum tins to hold our batter. If you cannot find these, you can use common soufflé or crème brûlée ramekins. (Be sure to get dishes that hold approximately 4-ounces of batter.) Another alternative is to purchase a six cup, disposable aluminum muffin pan and cut the aluminum into six individual cups.

1. Preheat oven to 450 degrees.
2. Sift together the cocoa powder and 1/8 cup flour for preparing the molds twice. Spray and then dust the foil cups or ramekins

with the cocoa and flour mixture. (This method is essentially the same as that used for preparing soufflé ramekins. It ensures that the delicate cakes will unmold cleanly.)
3. Melt butter and chocolate together over a double boiler.
4. In a separate bowl, whisk together yolks and whole eggs.
5. Sift the powdered sugar and flour together in a mixing bowl.
6. Whisk the egg mixture into the warm chocolate/butter mixture.
7. Whisk in the dry ingredients.
8. Divide batter into prepared cups.
9. Chill until needed.
10. Bake cakes for 9 to 11 minutes, or until the cakes begin to crown, yet the center is not set.
11. Carefully remove from the oven. Invert each cake onto the plate on which it will be served and remove tin. Garnish as desired and serve immediately.

FOR THE CHOCOLATE SAUCE:
For our chocolate sauce, Kelly starts with a caramel base and then enriches it with cocoa powder and vanilla bean simple syrup.

1. In a heavy-bottomed pot, combine sugar, corn syrup, and enough water to create a "wet sand" texture. Be sure there are no dry pockets of sugar. If necessary, wet down the sides of the pot with a pastry brush to remove any sugar crystals.
2. Over high heat, cook the sugar undisturbed until it begins to color around the edges of the pot. Swirl the sugar to evenly distribute the heat. Cook until light amber.
3. As soon as the sugar reaches the desired color, carefully pour in the cream. Reduce the heat to medium and whisk slowly until the caramel has melted and is smooth.

Continued on next page

VANILLA BEAN SIMPLE SYRUP

½ cup water

½ cup granulated sugar

½ vanilla bean, split and scraped

TOFFEE

16 tablespoons unsalted butter, cubed

¼ cup water

¼ cup light corn syrup

1¼ cups granulated sugar

2 teaspoons vanilla extract

STRAWBERRY DUST

2 pints strawberries

2 tablespoons granulated sugar

4. Add the butter, cocoa powder and salt. Whisk for 5 minutes over low heat.

5. Remove from the heat and stir in the vanilla extract and Vanilla Bean Simple Syrup.

6. Strain and chill the sauce in an ice bath. Refrigerate until needed. Good for 2 weeks.

FOR THE VANILLA BEAN SIMPLE SYRUP:

1. Combine water, sugar, and the vanilla bean pod and seeds; stir.

2. Bring to a boil and boil only until sugar is completely dissolved. Remove from heat.

FOR THE TOFFEE:

1. Combine all ingredients and bring to a boil.

2. Reduce heat to medium-low.

3. Cook until toffee registers 300 degrees on a candy thermometer.

4. Pour the hot mixture onto a Silpat.

5. Allow the toffee to cool to room temperature (approximately 1 hour).

6. Crush and store in an airtight container until needed. When ready to use, sprinkle around cake on the plate.

FOR THE STRAWBERRY DUST:

1. Wash and dry berries. Remove stems.

2. Slice as thinly as possible using a Japanese mandoline.

3. Arrange the slices on a Silpat set in a sheet pan. Be sure the slices do not touch.

4. Sprinkle the slices with a light dusting of sugar.

5. Bake in a 200-degree oven for approximately 1 hour, or until the chips are crisp when cool.

6. Place cooled chips in a coffee grinder.

7. Grind until fine and powdery.

8. Store airtight until needed. When ready to use, sprinkle around cake on the plate.

YIELDS 6 (4-OUNCE) CAKES

AUTUMN-SPICED DESSERT SPRING ROLLS

½ cup granulated sugar, divided
3 Granny Smith apples, peeled, cored, and diced
3 Bosc Pears, peeled, cored, and diced
¼ teaspoon ground cinnamon
¼ teaspoon ground cardamom
¼ teaspoon ground ginger
¼ teaspoon ground allspice

¼ teaspoon ground nutmeg
Pinch of fine sea salt
Spring roll wrappers
Canola oil

MINT SYRUP
¼ cup fresh mint leaves, tightly packed
⅛ cup fresh spinach leaves

½ cup corn syrup
1 ounce Rumple Minze Peppermint Schnapps

GRANNY SMITH APPLE CHIPS
2 cups granulated sugar
2 cups water
Juice of 2 lemons
1 Granny Smith apple

As the flavors of summer fade, apples and pears, cinnamon and cardamom replace the peaches and watermelons and strawberries of the previous season. To celebrate this transition and have a little fun, Kelly does what we do to almost everything in the South and fires up the fryer. Spice is the star here. Serve these piping hot spring rolls with cinnamon ice cream to wrap yourself even tighter in those fall flavors.

1. Add 1 tablespoon sugar to a hot sauté pan set over medium heat and allow it to melt. Then add the remaining sugar in small increments, allowing each addition of the sugar to melt fully before adding the next. Stir with a wooden spoon as necessary. Continue this process until all the sugar has been added and cooked to a deep amber.
2. Carefully add the diced apples and pears. The fruit shocks the caramel and keeps it from burning. Stir to evenly distribute the fruit in the caramel.
3. Add in the spices and salt and continue cooking and stirring intermittently until the liquid in the pan reduces to a thin syrup.
4. Pour the fruit and pan juices into a bowl, wrap, and refrigerate until cool.
5. When cool, strain off the excess liquid.
6. Roll the fruit in the spring rolls as described in the recipe for Beef Spring Rolls (see p. 66).
7. Fry in 350-degree canola oil until golden brown.
8. Drain on paper towels for 1 minute, slice on the bias, and serve with cinnamon caramel sauce, mint syrup, cinnamon ice cream, and an apple chip.

FOR THE MINT SYRUP:
1. Blanch mint and spinach for 15 seconds in boiling water. Remove the wilted leaves from the boiling water and shock immediately in ice water.
2. Remove leaves from water and squeeze in cloths to remove as much moisture as possible.
3. Purée mint, spinach, corn syrup and Rumple Minze until very smooth; strain.

FOR THE GRANNY SMITH APPLE CHIPS:
1. Preheat oven to 200 degrees.
2. Combine the sugar and water in a small pot. Bring to a boil and cook until sugar completely dissolves.
3. Remove from heat and cool in an ice bath.
4. Combine lemon juice and syrup.
5. Using an electric slicer or Japanese mandoline, cut apples latitudinally into 1/16-inch-thick slices.
6. Pour the lemon simple syrup over the apple slices.
7. Working quickly, shake as much excess syrup from the slices as possible and place in a single layer—not allowing them to touch—on a non-stick baking mat set in a sheet pan. Bake until dry and crisp, approximately 1 hour.
8. Remove the pan from the oven. Peel the chips from the mat. (If the chips crisp up too quickly and break, briefly return the pans to the oven.)
9. Store in an airtight container until needed.

YIELDS APPROXIMATELY 8 SPRING ROLLS

cooking techniques

Following is a list of general techniques used in recipes throughout the book:

BASTING

Basting is the process of spooning or brushing cooking food with melted butter, fat, and/or meat drippings. This additional fat keeps the surface of the food from drying out and aids in flavoring and coloring. Basting can also be done with the addition of fresh herbs and garlic to the basting liquid.

BLANCHING

Blanching is the process of cooking vegetables quickly in boiling, salted water and then shocking them quickly in ice water to stop the cooking. This process allows the vegetables to retain their vibrant colors (green, orange, yellow, etc.). Blanching also allows the vegetables to retain their natural density, or the slight resemblance of still being raw. Blanching vegetables can be done up to a day in advance. When the time comes to finish the vegetables, the colors remain bright.

STEPS AND TIPS:
- Bring a large pot of salted water to a boil.
- Have a large bowl of ice water ready.
- Blanch vegetables in small batches; this allows the water to continue boiling.
- Using a skimmer allows fast removal of the food from the boiling water.
- Plunge the vegetables in the ice water to stop the cooking process.
- Drain the vegetables well and place on paper towels to dry. Cover and refrigerate until ready to cook.

BRAISING

Braising is a technique that typically utilizes tougher, less costly cuts of meat. This cooking method is a two-part process. The first part involves browning by way of direct heat. The second part is the addition of liquid and cooking slowly at a low heat. The remaining liquid can then be reduced to form a sauce.

STEPS AND TIPS:
- Always use a cooking pan that can be placed in an oven.
- Cook protein by a high heat source to provide a caramelized surface. Commonly, browning is done in a large pan on the stove top with a small amount of oil. For more cumbersome pieces like lamb shanks, they can be coated in oil and caramelized quickly in a hot oven.
- After browning, use just enough liquid to cover the meat by three-fourths and no more. Use a tight fitting lid over the pan, or wrap with aluminum foil.
- Cook at a low temperature for a long period of time, preferably 250 degrees. You want the liquid inside to stay at a low simmer, making the meat turn out tender and moist. High heat cooks quickly, but makes the meat tough and dry.
- Cool the meat in the cooking liquid so that it will stay moist. Pulling the meat out prematurely causes the release of steam—moisture that should be in the meat to keep it moist.
- Remove the meat from the liquid when cold. Reduce the liquid to make the sauce.
- Reheat the meat with a small amount of sauce at a temperature no higher than 300 degrees. Serve with the finished sauce.

PAN ROASTING

This process is much more "hands-on" than just roasting. Pan roasting combines various cooking techniques into one and differs from roasting as it is done on the stovetop. This process starts by searing the food on both sides over medium-high heat. Then lower the temperature to medium and continuously flip the food from side to side every minute, making sure that it cooks evenly on both sides. It then goes to basting and finishes with resting.

STEPS AND TIPS:
- Dry the exterior of the meat with paper towels.
- Season the meat with salt and pepper on both sides. Salt pulls moisture out of the meat, drying the top layer.
- Prior to pan roasting, let the meat sit at room temperature—depending on thickness, approximately 20 minutes.
- Lightly pat the surface dry on both sides before cooking.
- Moisture creates steam and steam prevents a good sear.
- Allow a pan to get hot over medium-high heat. Add oil to the hot pan; you want the oil to be hot, but not smoking. High heat will cause the meat to brown too quickly and may burn.
- When the meat can be shaken free, it is time to flip it and repeat the process.
- Continuously flip the meat to ensure even cooking.

- Baste the meat with butter, fat, and/or meat drippings.
- Rest the meat when it is finished cooking.

RESTING

This is the process of cooling a cooked, roasted, or grilled piece of meat to a lower temperature. Resting allows the internal moisture to redistribute evenly, producing a moist finished product. This is a crucial step prior to cutting and carving. If you cut or carve when hot, all the juices will be forced violently out of the meat.

STEPS AND TIPS:

- Remove the item from the hot pan or cooking source and place on a large platter.
- The size of the item will determine the resting time required. The larger the item, the longer resting is required.

ROASTING

This is the process of cooking uncovered in the oven. This technique produces a well-browned exterior and a moist interior.

STEPS AND TIPS:

- Preheat the oven to 325 to 375 degrees (the best temperatures for this technique).
- Check the temperature with an oven thermometer and adjust heat as needed.
- Keep the oven rack in the center of the oven. This prevents burning the top and burning the bottom.
- Dry the exterior of the food with paper towels.
- Rub the entire surface evenly with a small amount oil. This allows proper heat transfer.
- Season the item with salt and pepper. Salt pulls moisture out, drying the top layer.
- Rest the item when it is finished cooking. The size will determine the time you want it to rest.

SAUTÉ

This is the process of cooking food quickly on the stovetop in a small amount of oil. High heat is used throughout the cooking. The word "sauté" translates to "jump in the pan."

STEPS AND TIPS:

- Allow a pan to get hot over high heat. Then add the oil to the hot pan; you want the oil to be hot, but not smoking.
- Add the food to the pan. It will jump around, so watch it closely.
- The food will change colors, becoming gradually darker.

SEARING

This is the process of forming a crust on the surface very quickly. It is done with a high degree of heat and a small amount of oil. It can be done in numerous ways—in a pan, in the oven, on a grill, or under a broiler. The oil acts to distribute the heat evenly.

STEPS AND TIPS:

- Season the meat with salt and pepper on both sides. Salt pulls moisture out, drying the top layer.
- Let the meat sit at room temperature—depending on thickness, about 20 minutes.
- Lightly pat the surface dry on both sides with paper towels before cooking. Moisture creates steam and steam prevents a good sear.
- Allow a pan to get hot over medium-high heat. Add the oil to the hot pan; you want the oil to be hot, but not smoking.
- High heat will cause the product to brown too quickly and may burn.
- When the meat can be shaken free, it is time to flip it and repeat the process.

SWEATING

Sweating is the process of allowing a vegetable to release its natural sugars while cooking slowly. Sweating will intensify the flavor of the item. Take care to keep the food moving around so that it doesn't cook too quickly in any one spot.

STEPS AND TIPS:

- Allow a pan to get hot over medium heat. Add oil, wait a couple of seconds and add the vegetables.
- Keep the pan moving. You should start to see a small amount of moisture in the pan.
- If the color starts to darken, turn the temperature down.

TESTING AND MEASUREMENTS

TESTING FOR DONENESS

The most simple and reliable way to test meat for doneness is to insert an instant-read thermometer into the thickest part of the meat. Wait 30 seconds before checking the temperature. Following is a chart of universal doneness temperatures, as well as the temperature the meat will reach after resting and the USDA recommended cooking temperatures.

TEMP.	CUT	REMOVE	AFTER RESTING	USDA
BLUE				
	Steak	115-120	115-120	N/A
	Chop	110-115	115-120	N/A
RARE				
	Steak/Chop	120-130	125-130	140
	Roast	115-120	125-130	140
MEDIUM RARE				
	Steak/ Chop	130-135	130-140	150
	Roast	125-130	130-140	150
MEDIUM				
	Steak/Chop	135-150	140-150	160
	Roast	130-140	140-150	160
MEDIUM WELL				
	Steak/Chop	150-165	155-165	170
	Roast	145-155	150-165	170
WELL				
	Roast	165	170-185	170

*Steak and Chop refers to cuts thinner than 1 1/4-inch thick. Cuts thicker than that should follow roast guidelines.

DRY OR WEIGHT MEASURES (APPROXIMATE)

1 ounce	
2 ounces	
3 ounces	
4 ounces	1/4 pound
8 ounces	1/2 pound
12 ounces	3/4 pound
16 ounces	1 pound
32 ounces	2 pounds
1 kilogram	2.2 pounds

LIQUID OR VOLUME MEASURES (APPROXIMATE)

1/4 teaspoon	=		
1/2 teaspoon	=		
1 teaspoon	=	1/3 tablespoon	
1 tablespoon	=	1/2 fluid ounce	3 teaspoons
2 tablespoons	=	1 fluid ounce	1/8 cup
1/4 cup	=	2 fluid ounces	4 tablespoons
1/3 cup	=	2 2/3 fluid ounces	5 1/3 tablespoons
1/2 cup	=	4 fluid ounces	8 tablespoons
2/3 cup	=	5 1/3 fluid ounces	10 2/3 tablespoons
3/4 cup	=	6 fluid ounces	12 tablespoons
7/8 cup	=	7 fluid ounces	14 tablespoons
1 cup	=	8 fluid ounces	16 tablespoons
2 cups	=	16 fluid ounces	32 tablespoons
4 1/4 cups	=	34 fluid ounces	
		.034 fluid ounce	1 cc
1 pint	=	16 fluid ounces	2 cups
2 pint	=	32 fluid ounces	1 quart
4 quarts	=	128 fluid ounces	1 gallon
1 liter	=	1.057 quarts	1/4 gallon

wine pairings

Cold Oysters	C. Moreau Chablis—crisp wine with juicy lime and grapefruit flavors and good minerality
Tuna and Oysters	d'Arenberg "Hermit Crab" Marsanne-Viognier, McLaren Vale—exotic aromas and flavors of marmalade, white flowers and lychee nut
Tuna Tartare	Rochioli Sauvignon Blanc, Russian River Valley—a medium-bodied wine with flavors of melon and fig and lively acidity
Beef Tartare	Loring Pinot Noir "Gary's Vineyard," Santa Lucia Highlands—velvety texture on the palate with raspberry, cherry, pepper and earth flavors
Deconstructed Spicy Tuna Roll	Salomon Riesling "Steinterrassen," Austria—intense citrus fruit and stony mineral character with a long fine, dry finish
Thai Coconut Chicken	Hiedler Gruner Veltliner, Kamptal—orange and lemon zest flavors on the palate with notes of fresh herb, pepper and stone
Bay Scallop Ceviche	Sherwood Estate Sauvignon Blanc, Marlborough—a floral refined nose with fresh lemon and gooseberry flavors and good acidity
Steamed Squash Blossoms	La Craie Vouvray—aromas of honey and pears with a waxy texture and bright acidity along with an Old World-style mustiness
Benne Seed Shrimp	L'Ecole No. 41 Chardonnay, Columbia Valley—a medium-bodied wine with apple and spice aromas and fresh white fruit flavors
Oysters and Caviar	Chateau Carbonieux, Pessac-Leognan—great balance of crisp acidity and rich texture; fig and citrus aromas with lemon and apricot flavors
Foie Gras	Tokaji Aszu Disnoko 5 Puttonyos—concentrated and sweet, with apricot and pineapple flavors along with notes of ginger-cinnamon and honey; full bodied and deep gold in color
Crab Cakes	Patricia Green "Four Winds" Chardonnay, Yamhill County—aromas of candied lemons and apple followed by a great balance of vibrant acidity and intense rich fruit
Vietnamese Spring Rolls	Qupe Syrah, Central Coast—bright style with ripe cherry and currants balanced with pepper and some herbs

Butter-Poached Lobster	Leeuwin Chardonnay "Artist Series," Margaret River—butter, orange, honeysuckle, and pear flavors with discernable, but not overpowering notes of oak in the background
Scallops and Bacon	Brickhouse Gamay Noir, Willamette Valley—dark fruit flavor, cassis and black currant, licorice notes and a touch of spice
Lobster Bisque	Melville Chardonnay, Santa Rita Hills—fresh style, framed with good minerality, honeysuckle and tropical fruits
Caesar Salad	Mulderbosch Sauvignon Blanc, Stellenbosch—intense nose of white pear and lime, concentrated flavors of grapefruit, gooseberry and citrus
Almond-Fried Goat Brie	Fournier Grand Cuvee Sancerre—a fresh, aromatic nose; lime and kiwi flavors with refreshing acidity and a crisp, dry finish
Arugula Salad	Herve Seguin Pouilly-Fume—smoky mineral and citrus aromas, flavors of ripe apple and pear and a long finish
Portobello Mille-feulle	Vina Sastre Ribera del Duero—aroma of truffles, earth and crushed fruit; soft on the palate with bright fruit and oak notes
Filet with Boursin Cheese	Frescobaldi "Montesodi" Chianti Rufina—full-bodied, modern style, vanilla and spice aromas, sweet plum fruit and elegant tannins
Miso Chicken	Andrew Murray "Enchante" Rousanne-Marsanne, Santa Ynez—medium-bodied aromas of citrus blossoms with ripe melon, honeysuckle and apricot flavors
Duck Au Poivre	Cliff Lede Claret, Stag's Leap District—full-bodied wine with plum, chocolate and toast on the nose followed by ripe cherry, currant and dark chocolate flavors
Short Rib and Lobster	Shafer Cabernet Sauvignon, Napa (375 ml)—juicy blackberry and cherry fruit with notes of herbs, cedar, and black pepper
Steak Diane	Chateau Gloria, St. Julien—smoky nose of black cherry, black olive and cedar, lush on the palate with sweet blueberry and currant
Smoked Salmon Wellington	Langhe "Freedom Hill" Pinot Noir, Willamette Valley—black cherry and boysenberry flavors on the palate with notes of briar and earth; crisp acidity to add freshness to the rich fruit

Maple-Lacquered Quail	Alvaro Palacios "Les Terrasses" Priorat—rich and smooth on the palate with ripe blackberry, plum, dark chocolate, licorice and tobacco flavors.
Szechwan Peppercorn Encrusted Tuna	"Goat-Roti" Charles Back Shiraz-Viognier, Western Cape—smoky, meaty nose with dark raspberry, licorice and black pepper
Crisp Wasabi Tuna	Zind-Humbrecht Riesling, Alsace—rich texture with pineapple and stone aromas followed by citrus and honeydew flavors and good acidity
Shrimp and Sausage	Kaesler "Avignon" Grenache Blend, Barossa Valley—full-bodied red, sweet cherry, strawberry along with fresh herbs and pepper
Serrano Wrapped Mahi-mahi	Soave Classico Pra "Monte Grande"—Medium-bodied with good minerality; apple, pear and almond on the nose with more tropical flavors of tangerine and lemon on the palate
Châteaubriand	Paul Hobbs "El Felino" Malbec, Mendoza—lush and ripe, blackberry and boysenberry with mocha and spice silky finish
Rack of Lamb	Vilafonte "Series M," South Africa—nose of red plums, black raspberries and spice with bright red fruit flavors that are soft on the palate
Hamiachi	Schloss Gobelsburg Gruner Veltliner "Steinsetz," Kamptal—fresh fruit aromas with a lean in texture and strong minerality that is bright and juicy on the palate with notes of wet stone and peach
Wok-Seared Squid	Domain Ostertag Muscat "Fronholz," Alsace—fresh perfumed aromas of lime zest and mint, clean peachy flavors with a dry finish
Duck Confit and Foie Gras	Felton Road Pinot Noir, Central Otago—aromas of ripe berries, herbs and spices, soft texture with a great blend of raspberry, strawberry and earth
Thai Seafood Salad	Icardi Cortese "L'Aurora"—delicate aromas of flower blossom, anise and white pepper, fresh peach and citrus on the palate with a clean finish
Seared Golden Tilefish	K Viognier, Napa—a crisp wine with pear and peach flavors and good acidity and mineral character
Bacon and Oyster Stew	J.J. Prum Wehlener Sonnenuhr Riesling Spatlese—focused, medium-bodied white with strong slate minerality, intense lime and apricot flavors

Asian Chicken Noodle Soup	Ponzi Pinot Gris, Willamette Valley—complex aromas of ripe apple, pear and apricot as well as on the palate and crisp finish
Roasted Oysters	C. Moreau Chablis—crisp wine with juicy lime and grapefruit flavors and good minerality
Salad Nicoise	Costieres de Nimes Rose Chateau Mas Neuf—fresh flavors and aromas of strawberry, watermelon and raspberry in a refreshing format
Seared Duck and Watercress	J. Palacios Bierzo—spicy aromas of nutmeg and cinnamon along with cherry and blueberry; a silky mouthful
Braised Wreckfish	Icario Vino Nobile di Montepulciano—a bright, medium-bodied wine; aromas and flavors of red berry and plum with a touch of smoke
Grilled Wahoo	Littorai Pinot Noir, Sonoma Coast—vibrant nose of strawberry and cranberry; well-balanced ripe fruit on the palate with earth notes
Palmetto Bass	Rudd Sauvignon Blanc, Napa—a crisp wine with good acidity and flavors of fresh figs, melons, grapefruit, and lemon grass
Grilled Swordfish	Perrin & Fils "Les Sinards" Chateauneuf-du-Pape—full-bodied, ripe style with candied fruits along with smoke and leather

Sources

Anson Mills
1922-C Gervais Street
Columbia, South Carolina 29201
www.ansonmills.com
803-467-4122
Grits, hominy, polenta, and Carolina
gold rice

Korin Japanese Trading Corp.
57 Warren Street
New York, New York 10007
800-626-2172
212-587-7021
www.korin.com or
www.japanese-knife.com
Knives, water stones, mandolins,
service ware

Foods in Season
866-767-2464
www.foodsinseason.com
Baby shiitake mushrooms

Mikuni Wild Harvest
866-993-9927
www.mikuniwildharvest.com
Tahitian vanilla beans, truffles

The Chef's Garden, Inc.
9009 Huron-Avery Road
Huron, Ohio 44839
800-289-4644
www.chefsgarden.com
Micro greens, squash blossoms,
beans and peas

J.B. Prince Company
36 East 31st Street
New York, New York 10016-6821
800-473-0577
www.jbprince.com
Crème brûlée dishes, soufflé ramekins

Sur La Table
800-243-0852
www.surlatable.com
Stainless and copper cookware

Williams-Sonoma
877-812-6235
www.williams-sonoma.com
Microplane, Swiss peeler, ISI canister

Quail International, Inc.
1940 Highway 15 South
Greensboro, Georgia 30642
800-843-3204
www.plantationquail.net
Quail

Norpac Fisheries Export
1535 Colburn Street
Honolulu, Hawaii 96817
808-842-3474
www.norpacexport.com
Tuna, swordfish

Hudson Valley Foie Gras
80 Brooks Road
Ferndale, New York 12734
845-292-2500
www.hudsonvalleyfoiegras.com
Foie gras, Magret duck breast

Split Creek Farm
3806 Centerville Road
Anderson, South Carolina 29625
864-287-3921
www.splitcreek.com
Fromage blanc, feta, chevre logs

Ashley Farms
4787 Kinnamon Road
Winston-Salem, North Carolina 27103
336-766-9900
www.ashleyfarms.com
Whole chickens, turkeys and duck

Bell & Evans
P.O. Box 39
154 West Main Street
Fredricksburg, Pennsylvania 17026
717-865-6626
www.bellandevans.com
Whole chickens, turkeys and ducks

Black Creek Apiaries
Hartsville, South Carolina
Seasonal Honey

Kennerty Farms
John's Island, South Carolina
843-559-1179
Baby lettuces, asian greens, asparagus,
potatoes, and root vegetables

Index

Aioli, Roasted Garlic: 91; in Lobster BLT, 81

Almond-Fried Goat Brie with Cranberry-Walnut Chutney and Bitter Greens, **88**-89; wine for, 247

Alvaro Palacios "Les Terrasses" Priorat, 248

Andrew Murray "Enchante" Rousanne-Marsanne, 247

Apples, Granny Smith, 237

Artichokes: with Grilled Swordfish, 146; Jerusalem, with Szechwan Pepper Crusted Tuna, 149; cocktail, with Pan-Roasted Chicken, 159; preparing, 204-5

Arugula: in Hamiachi with Cucumber Noodles, 49; in Truffle Essence Arugula, 57; Salad with Walnut Vinaigrette, Goat Cheese and Toasted Walnuts, **86**-87

Arugula Salad, 87; wine for, 247

Asian Beef Salad with Sour Soy Vinaigrette, **96**-97

Asian Chicken Noodle Soup, 116; wine for, 249

Asian Tuna Tartare with Cucumbers, Chili Glaze, Shiitake Mushrooms and Chinese Flatbread, **39**, **42**-43, **45**; wine for, 246

Asparagus: with Shallots and Garlic, 128; with Serrano Wrapped Mahi-Mahi and Shrimp, 137; Sautéed, 176, 189

Autumn-Spiced Dessert Spring Rolls, **236**-37

Avocado and Soft-Shell Crab Roll with Black Spanish Radish and Black Bean Soy, **70**-71

Bacon: in Bacon Braised Greens, 165; in Choucroute, 171; with Brussel Sprouts, 202

Bacon, Braised: 69; with Lobster BLT, 81

Bacon and Oyster Stew, 116; wine for, 248

Bacon Braised Greens, 165

Balsamic syrup, 92

Balsamic Vinegar, Aged, 100

Basil Oil: 24; in Crab Cakes, 57; in Chilled Tomato Soup, 117; with Grilled Swordfish, 147

Bass, hybrid, 145

Basting, 240

Bay Scallop Ceviche with Grape Tomatoes, Coriander and Lime, 46; wine for, 246

Beans: black, soy, 22; dragon, 91; romano, 91; waxed, 91; Beans, Butter, 202

Beans, green. See Haricots verts.

Béarnaise Sauce: 189; with Châteaubriand, 173

Beef Spring Rolls, 66

Beef Tartare with Brioche Toast Points and Olive Oil, 49; wine for, 246

Beef Tenderloins: in Asian Beef Salad, 97; in Châteaubriand, 173; in Grilled Filet of Beef, 175-76

Beef short ribs, 185

Beets, Roasted: 159; with Braised Lamb Shanks, 199

Belgian endive, braised, 149

Benne Seed Shrimp, **76**-77; wine for, 246

Beurre Fondue: 113; with Oysters and Caviar, 55; with Butter-Poached Lobster, 78; with Lobster BLT, 81; with Thai Spiced Short Ribs and Lobster, 185-86

Bisque, Lobster, 113

Black Bean Soy, 22; with Avocado and Soft-Shell Crab Roll, 71

Black Olive Oil, 91

Black Spanish Radish, 71

Blanching, 240

Blood Orange Vinaigrette, 159

Blueberry Compote, Gingered, 223

Bok Choy, Baby, 161

Boursin Cheese: 175; with Portobello Mille-Feulle, 101

Braised Bacon: 69; with Lobster BLT, 81

Braised Belgian Endive, 149

Braised Lamb Shanks with Roquefort Polenta and Roasted Beets, **198**-99

Braised Wreckfish with Eggplant, Baby Squash, Tomatoes and Crispy Squash Blossom, **132**-33; wine for, 249

Braising, 240

Bratwurst, 171

Brickhouse Gamay Noir, 247

Brie, goat, 89

Brioche Toast Points, 49, 100

Broth, Shellfish, 138

Brussel Sprouts with Bacon Shallots and Garlic, 202

Butter: tips for using, 25; Squash Blossom, 25; Lemon, 25; Truffle, 26; Herb, 26; Clarified, 26; Ginger-Soy, 56

Butter beans, 202

Butternut Squash Risotto, 156

Butternut Squash Soup with Duck Confit, Pecans, Fresh Nutmeg and Maple Syrup, **118**-19

Butter-Poached Lobster with Truffle Grits Cake and Lobster Glaçage, 78; wine for, 247

C. Moreau Chablis, 246, 249

Caesar Salad, 247

Capers: with mizuna, 149; with raisins in compote, 177

Caramel, Soy, 155

Caramelized Fennel, 177, 202

Caramelized Rice Krispies, 221

Caviar, with Oysters and Melted Leeks and Chervil, 55

Celery Root Purée, 185

Ceviche, Bay Scallop, 46

Chanterelles, 75

Château Carbonieux, 246

Château Gloria, 247

Château Potatoes: 173, with rack of lamb, 197

Châteaubriand, with Château Potatoes, Haricots Verts, Béarnaise and Madeira Sauces, **172**-73; wine for, 248

Cheese, boursin: with Portobello Mille-Feulle, 101;with filet of beef, 175-76

Cheese, feta: with seared duck, 92; with mizuna and capers, 149

Cheese, goat: with Arugula Salad, 87; in goat brie, with bitter greens, 89; with dried fig compote, 100; in Boursin Cheese, 175; in English Pea Risotto, 193; in grits, 208-9; honeyed, 227

Cheese, Gruyère, in Potato Fondue, 127

Cheesecake, Key Lime White Chocolate, **222**-23

Cherry: in Ginger-Cherry Compote, 65

Chervil, fresh, 55, 113

Chicken: in stock, 32; in Thai Coconut Chicken, 109; in Asian Chicken Noodle Soup, 116; Miso, 155; Lemon-Rosemary Roasted, 157; Pan-Roasted, 159-60

Chicken Noodle Soup, Asian, 116

Chicken Stock: 32; in Thai Coconut Chicken, 109; in Asian Chicken Noodle Soup, 116

Chili Garlic Glaze: 23; with Crisp Wasabi Tuna, 131

Chili Glaze: 22; in Asian Tuna Tartare, 43; with Benne Seed Shrimp, 77

Chili Soy Sauce: 22; in Wok-Seared Squid, 67; with Edamame and Shiitake Mushrooms, 131, 139; with Miso Chicken, 155

Chilled Pea Soup with Lobster and Mint Vinaigrette, **120**-121

Chilled Tomato Soup with Lump Crab and Basil Oil, 117

Chinese Five Spice Powder: 23; with Maple-Lacquered Quail, 156

Chinese Flatbread, 43

Chive Oil: 24; with Scallops and Braised Bacon, 69; in Butternut Squash Soup, 119; with Maple-Lacquered Quail, 156; in Blood Orange Vinaigrette, 159

Chocolate Peanut Butter Caramel Cake, **216**-19

Chocolate Sauce, 232-33

Choucroute, 171

Chutney, Cranberry-Walnut, 89

Cilantro Lime Glaze, 41

Citrus Soy: 22; in Asian Beef Salad, 97

Clams, Littleneck, 138

Clarified Butter: 26; in Lobster Glaçage, 78; in Portobello Mille-Feulle, 101; in Smoked Salmon Wellington, 128

Cliff Lede Claret, 247

Cocktail Sauce, Green Tomato-Wasabi, 47, 56

Coconut Cream, 109

Collard greens, 165

Compote: Ginger-Cherry, 65; Dried Fig, 100; Raisin Caper, 177; Gingered Blueberry, 224

Confit: Lemon, 27, 157; Duck, 65; Potato, 146-47

Coriander Pork with Caramelized Fennel and Raisin Caper Compote, 177

Corn Fricassee, 129

Corn Muffins, 59

Corn Purée, 57, 129

Corn Stock: 32; in Corn Purée, 57, 129

Costieres de Nimes Rose Chateau Mas Neuf, 249

Crabs, soft-shell: in Soft-Shell Crab Rolls, 71; in Tempura Soft-Shell Crab, 189-90

Crab Cakes with Truffle Essence Arugula and Sweet Corn Purée, 57

Crabmeat: jumbo: in Crab Cakes, 57; lump, in Thai Seafood Salad, 102; lump, in Chilled Tomato Soup, 117

Cranberry-Walnut Chutney, 89

Crème Brûlée, Green Tea, 221

Crimini mushrooms, 127, 181

Crisp Wasabi Tuna with Edamame, Baby Shiitake Mushrooms and Chili Garlic glaze, **130**-31; wine for, 248

Croutons, garlic, 93

Crushed Red Potatoes, 203

Cucumbers: with Asian Tuna Tartare, 43; in Cucumber Lime Mignonette, 47; Noodles, 49

Cucumber Lime Mignonette, 47

Cucumber Noodles, 49

Cypress Caesar Salad, 93

D'Arenberg "Hermit Crab" Marsanne-Viognier, 246

Daikon radish, 97

Deconstructed Lamb T-Bone with English Pea Risotto, **192**-94

Deconstructed Spicy Tuna Roll, 48; wine for, 246

Domain Ostertag Muscat "Fronholz", 248

Dragon beans, 91

Dried Fig Compote, 100

Dry spices: in Chinese Five Spice Powder, 23; tips for using, 27

Duck Au Poivre, 161

Duck Confit, 65; in Butternut Squash Soup, 119

Duck Confit and Foie Gras with Leeks, Mizuna and Ginger-Cherry Compote, **64**-65; wine for, 248

Duck Legs, 65, 119

Duck Stock: 33; in Shallot Pecan Jus, 156; in Magret Duck Au Poivre, 161

Duck, seared, with Watercress, 000: with Feta, Dried Figs and Balsamic Syrup, 92

Duxelles, 127

Edamame: with Baby Shiitake Mushrooms, 131, 139; with Palmetto Bass, 145; with Thai Spiced Short Ribs and Lobster, 185-86

Eggplant, Japanese, Baby Squash and Tomatoes, 133

Endive, Braised Belgian, 149

English Pea Risotto, 193

Escarole, in Bacon Braised Greens, 165

Felton Road Pinot Noir, 248

Fennel, Baby, 138

Fennel, Caramelized, 177, 203

Feta cheese: with seared duck, 92; with mizuna and capers, 149

Figs, dried: with seared duck, 92; in compote, 100

Fine Sea Salt, 23

Fish Fumet: 34; with Bacon and Oyster

Stew, 116; with Braised Wreckfish, 133

Flatbread, Chinese, 43

Fleur de Sel (salt), 23

Foie Gras: Seared, with Spiced Peaches and Corn Muffins, 59-60, 246; Salt-Cured, 61; in Smoked Salmon Wellington, 127;

Fondue: Beurre, 113; Gruyère Potato, 206

Fortified Stock, 34

Fournier Grand Cuvee Sancerre, 247

Frescobaldi "Montesodi" Chianti Rufina, 247

Fresh Oysters with Cucumber Lime Mignonette and Green Tomato-Wasabi Cocktail Sauce, 47; wine for, 246

Fricassee: Sweet Corn, 129; Succotash, 202

Fromage Blanc with Dried Fig Compote, Watercress and Aged Balsamic, 100. *See also* Goat Cheese

Fruit and Cheese, **226**-27

Garden and Herb Salad with Garlic Shallot Vinaigrette, **94**-95

Garlic and Herb Roasted Rack of Lamb with Château Potatoes, Haricots Verts and Balsamic Lamb Reduction, **196**-97

Garlic Croutons, 93

Garlic Shallot Vinaigrette, 89, 95

Ginger Pork, with Steamed Squash Blossoms, 75

Ginger-Cherry Compote, 65

Gingered Blueberry Compote, 223

Ginger-Soy Butter, 56

Glaçage, Lobster: 78

Glaze: Chili, 22; Chili Garlic, 23; Cilantro Lime, 41

Glazing Ganache, 218-19

Goat Cheese: with Arugula Salad, 87; in Boursin Cheese, 175; in English Pea Risotto, 193; in grits, 209; honeyed, 227

Goat Cheese Grits: 208-9; with Shrimp and Sausage, 141

"Goat-Roti" Charles Back Shiraz-Viognier, 248

Graham Crackers, Homemade, 223

Grains, types of, 27

Grand Marnier Crème Anglaise, 229-30

Grand Marnier Soufflé, **228**-30

Granny Smith Apple Chips, 237

Green beans. See Haricots verts

Green Tea Crème Brûlée, **220**-21

Green Tomato-Wasabi Cocktail Sauce, 47, 56

Greens, Asian, in Asian Beef Salad, 97

Greens, Bacon Braised, 165

Greens: bitter, 89; mixed, 95; washing of, 90. *See also* Arugula, Mizuna

Grilled Filet of Beef with Boursin Cheese, Asparagus, Fingerling Potatoes and Madeira Sauce, **174**-75; wine for, 247

Grilled Swordfish with Confit Potatoes, Artichokes and Lemon Butter, 146-47; wine for, 249

Grilled Wahoo with Sweet Corn Fricassee, Rock Shrimp and Lacy Potatoes, 129; wine for, 249

Grits Cakes, Truffle: with Butter-Poached Lobster, 78; with Serrano Wrapped Mahi-Mahi, 137

Grits, Goat Cheese: with Shrimp and Sausage, 141; making of, 208-9

Gruyere cheese for potato fondue, 206

Gruyère Cheese, 127

Gruyère Potato Fondue: 127, 206; with Roast Pork Shoulder, 171; with Steak Diane, 181

Ham, Serrano, with Mahi-Mahi, 137

Hamiachi with Cucumber Noodles, Arugula, Yuzu Soy and Pink Peppercorn, 48; wine for, 248

Haricots verts (green beans): in Salad Nicoise, 91; with Palmetto Bass, 145; with Miso Chicken, 155; with Châteaubriand, 173; with rack of lamb, 197

Herb Butter: 26; in Bacon Braised Greens, 165; with Steak Diane and Roasted Mushrooms, 181; with Brussel Sprouts, 202

Herb Oil, 25

Herbs: tips on, 23

Herve Sequin Pouille-Fume, 247

Hiedler Gruner Veltliner, 246

Homemade Graham Crackers, 223

Hominy: with Succotash Fricassee, 202; making of, 210-11

Honey Wheat Brioche: 227; for toast points, 49; with Lobster BLT, 81

Honeyed Goat Cheese, **226**-27

Icardi Cortese "L'Aurora", 248

Icario Vino Nobile di Montepulciano, 249

Infused Oil, 24

J. J. Prum Wehlener Sonnenuhr Riesling Spatlese, 248

J. Palacios Bierzo, 249

Jerusalem Artichokes, 149

JoAnn's Chocolate-Buttermilk Cake, 217

Jus: Shallot Pecan, 156; Natural, 164

K Viognier, 248

Kaesler "Avignon" Grenache Blend, 248

Key Lime White Chocolate Cheesecake, **222**-23

Kosher Salt, 23

Kumomoto Oysters, 41

L'Ecole No. 41 Chardonnay, 246

La Craie Vouvray, 246

Lacy Potatoes, 129

Lamb: saddle, 192-94; racks, 197; shanks, 199

Lamb Sausage, 141

Langhe "Freedom Hill" Pinot Noir, 247

Leeks, Melted, 55

Leeks, with Duck Confit and Foie Gras, 65

Leeks, with Short Ribs and Lobster, 185-86

Leeks with Shrimp and Sausage, 141

Leeuwin Chardonnay "Artist Series", 247

Lemon Beurre Blanc, 127

Lemon Butter: 25; with Palmetto Bass, 145; with Grilled Swordfish, 146-47; with Roasted Chicken, 157; in Caramelized Fennel, 177, 203

Lemon Confit, 27

Lemon-Rosemary Roasted Chicken, 157

Lettuce, washing, 90

Limes: in Cilantro Lime Glaze, 41; in Bay Scallop Ceviche, 46

Littorai Pinot Noir, 249

Lobster: Butter-Poached, 78; cooking

of, 79; in Lobster BLT, 81; in
   Bisque, 113; in Chilled Pea Soup,
   121; in Thai Spiced Short Ribs and
   Lobster, 185-86
Lobster "BLT" with Braised Bacon,
   Lobster Claw, Heirloom Tomato
   and Garlic Aioli, **80**-81
Lobster Bisque with Butter-Poached
   Lobster and Chervil, **112**-13; wine
   for, 247
Lobster Glaçage, 78
Loring Pinot Noir "Gary's Vineyard", 246
Lotus root, in Asian Beef Salad, 97

Madeira Sauce: 175; with
   Châteaubriand, 173
Magenta Lime Chips, 224
Magret Duck Au Poivre with Baby Bok
   Choy and Truffle Sweet Potatoes,
   161-**163**; wine for, 247
Mahi-Mahi, Serrano wrapped, 137
Maitake mushrooms, 155
Maldon Sea Salt, 23
Maple Syrup, in Butternut Squash
   Soup, 119
Maple-Lacquered Quail with Butternut
   Squash Risotto and Shallot Pecan
   Jus, 156; wine for, 248
Mascarpone: with Butternut Squash
   Risotto, 156; with honeyed goat
   cheese, 227
Measurements, 243
Melted Leeks, 55
Melville Chardonnay, 247
Mignonette, Cucumber Lime, 47
Mille-Feuille, 101
Mint Oil: 24; in Wok-Seared Squid, 67;
   in Thai Seafood Salad, 102; in Thai
   Coconut Chicken, 109; in Chilled
   Pea Soup with Lobster, 121; with
   Seared Tilefish, 139; with Shrimp
   and Sausage, 141
Mint Syrup, 237
Mint Vinaigrette, 121
Miso Chicken with Maitake
   Mushrooms, Green Beans and Soy
   Caramel, **154**-55; wine for, 247
Mizuna: with Duck Confit and Foie
   Gras, 65; in Asian Chicken Noodle
   Soup, 116; with capers, 149

Monkfish, in Seafood Pot, 138
Muffins, Corn, 59
Mulderbosch Sauvignon Blanc, 247
Mushrooms, chanterelles, 75
Mushrooms, crimini: in Smoked
   Salmon Wellington, 127; in
   Roasted Mushrooms, 181
Mushrooms, maitake, 155
Mushrooms, portobello: in Portobello
   Mille-Feulle, 101; in Smoked Sal-
   mon Wellington, 127; Roasted, 181
Mushrooms, shiitake: with Asian Tuna
   Tartare, 43; in Duck Confit and
   Foie Gras, 65; in Thai Coconut
   Chicken, 109; in Asian Chicken
   Noodle Soup, 116; in Smoked
   Salmon Wellington, 127; with
   Edamame and Wasabi Tuna, 131;
   with Edamame and Seared
   Tilefish, 139; Roasted, 181; with
   Thai-Spiced Short Ribs and
   Lobster, 185-86
Mussels, 138
Mustard greens, 165

New York strip steaks, 181

Oils: tips for using, 24; Infused, 24;
   Basil, 24; Mint, 24; Chive, 24;
   Herb, 24; Black Olive, 91
Orange, Blood, Vinaigrette, 159
Oysters, Fresh, with Cucumber Lime
   Mignonette and Green Tomato-
   Wasabi Cocktail Sauce, 47
Oysters, in Bacon and Oyster Stew, 116
Oysters, Kumomoto, with Sashimi
   Tuna with Cilantro Lime Glaze and
   Pineapple Wasabi, 41
Oysters, Roasted, with Green Tomato-
   Wasabi Cocktail Sauce and
   Ginger-Soy Butter, 56
Oysters, west coast: with Caviar and
   Melted Leeks and Chervil, 55
Oysters and Caviar with Melted Leeks
   and Chervil, **54**-55; wine for, 246

Palmetto Bass en Papillote with
   Summer Beans and Tomatoes,
   144-45; wine for, 249
Pan Roasting, 240-41

Pan-Roasted Chicken with Roasted
   Beets, Baby Artichokes and Blood
   Orange Vinaigrette, **158**-60
Pastas, types of, 27
Patricia Green "Four Winds"
   Chardonnay, 246
Paul Hobbs "El Felino" Malbec, 248
Peaches, Spiced, 59
Peanut Butter Caramel Mascarpone
   Filling, 217
Peanut-Cocoa Nib Brittle, 218-19
Pears, Bosc, 237
Peas, Crowder, in Succotash
   Fricassee, 202
Peas, English: in Chilled Pea Soup,
   121; in Risotto, 193
Pecans, in Butternut Squash Soup, 119
Perrin & Fils "Les Sinards"
   Chateauneuf-du-Pape, 249
Phyllo: in Portobello Mille-Feulle, 101;
   in Smoked Salmon Wellington,
   128; with Wasabi Tuna, 131
Pineapple Wasabi, 41
Polenta, Roquefort, 199
Ponzi Pinot Gris, 249
Pork: in stock, 34; braised, belly, 69;
   ginger, 75; Roast, Shoulder, 171;
   loins, Coriander, 177
Port Wine Syrup, 101
Portobello Mille-feulle, 247
Portobello mushrooms: with Mille-
   Feulle, 101; roasted, 181
Potato confit, with Grilled Swordfish,
   146-47
Potato Fondue, Gruyère: 127, 206; with
   Roast Pork Shoulder, 171
Potato Gratin, 206
Potatoes, Château: 173; with rack of
   lamb, 197
Potatoes, fingerling: with Potato Confit,
   146-47; with Filet of Beef, 175
Potatoes, red bliss: for Château
   Potatoes, 173; in Crushed Red
   Potatoes, 203
Potatoes, russet: in Lacy Potatoes,
   129; for Potato Gratin, 206
Potatoes, Yukon gold: in Gruyère
   Potato Fondue, 127, 206
Purée: Corn, 57, 129; Celery Root,
   185

Quail, Maple-Lacquered, 156
Quick Stock, 34
Qupe Syrah, 246

Rack of lamb, 197, 248
Radish: black Spanish or daikon, with
     Avocado and Soft-Shell Crab Roll,
     71; daikon, in Asian Beef Salad, 97
Raisin Caper Compote, 177
Resting, 242
Rice Foam, 48
Rice, carniroli or arborio: in Butternut
     Squash Risotto, 156; with
     Deconstructed Lamb T-Bone, 193
Rice: Carolina Gold: in Rice Foam, 48
Rice: types of, 27
Risotto: Butternut Squash, 156;
     English Pea, 193
Roast Pork Shoulder with Choucroute
     and Gruyère Potato Fondue, **170**-71
Roasted Beets, 159; with Braised
     Lamb Shanks, 199
Roasted Duck Stock, 33
Roasted Garlic Aioli, 91; with Lobster
     BLT, 81
Roasted Mushrooms, 181
Roasted Oysters with Green Tomato-
     Wasabi Cocktail Sauce and
     Ginger-Soy Butter, 56; wine for, 249
Roasting, 242
Rochioli Sauvignon Blanc, 246
Rock Salt, 23
Romaine hearts, 93
Romano beans, 91
Roquefort Polenta, 199
Roux, in Lobster Bisque, 113
Rudd Sauvignon Blanc, 249

Salad Nicoise with Summer Beans,
     Black Olive Oil and Roasted Garlic
     Aioli, **90**-91; wine for, 249
Salads: Duck Confit and Foie Gras with
     Leeks, Mizuna and Ginger-Cherry
     Compote, 65; Arugula with Walnut
     Vinaigrette, Goat Cheese and
     Toasted Walnuts, 87; Almond-
     Fried Goat Brie with Cranberry-
     Walnut Chutney and Bitter Greens,
     89; Salad Nicoise with Summer
     Beans, Black Olive Oil and Roasted

Garlic Aioli, 91; Seared Duck with
     Watercress with Feta, Dried Figs
     and Balsamic Syrup, 92; Cypress
     Caesar Salad, 93; Garden and Herb
     Salad with Garlic Shallot Vinaigrette,
     95; Asian Beef Salad with Sour Soy
     Vinaigrette, 97; Thai Seafood Salad,
     102
Salmon, Smoked, Wellington, 128
Salomon Riesling "Steinterrassen", 246
Salt-Cured Foie Gras, 61
Salts: types of, 23
Sashimi Tuna with Kumomoto Oysters
     with Cilantro Lime Glaze and
     Pineapple Wasabi, **40**-41. *See also*
     Tuna, sashimi
Sauce, chocolate, 233
Sauerkraut, with Choucroute, 171
Sautéing, 242
Scallops and Bacon, 247
Scallops and Braised Bacon with
     Succotash and Smoked Pork
     Reduction, **68**-69
Scallops, bay: in ceviche, 46; with
     Braised Bacon, 69
Schloss Gobelsburg Gruner Vletliner
     "Steinsetz", 248
Seafood Pot with Baby Fennel,
     Tomatoes and Shellfish Broth, 138
Seared Duck with Watercress with
     Feta, Dried Figs and Balsamic
     Syrup, 92; wine for, 249
Seared Foie Gras with Spiced Peaches
     and Corn Muffins, **58**-60
Seared Golden Tilefish with Edamame,
     Baby Shiitake Mushrooms and Thai
     Coconut Cream, 139; wine for, 248
Searing, 242
Sel Gris (salt), 23
Serrano Wrapped Mahi-Mahi with
     Truffle Grits, Asparagus, Grape
     Tomatoes and Sautéed Shrimp,
     136-37; wine for, 248
Shafer Cabernet Sauvignon, 247
Shallot Pecan Jus, 156
Shallot Vinaigrette, with Garlic, 89, 95
Shellfish Stock: 34; in Lobster
     Glaçage, 78; in Seafood Pot, 138;
     with Shrimp and Sausage, 141
Shiitake mushrooms: with Asian Tuna

Tartare, 43; in Duck Confit and
     Foie Gras, 65; in Thai Coconut
     Chicken, 109; in Asian Chicken
     Noodle Soup, 116; baby, with
     Edamame and Wasabi Tuna, 131;
     with Edamame and Seared
     Tilefish, 139; in Roasted
     Mushrooms, 181; in Thai Spiced
     Short Ribs and Lobster, 185-86
Shiso, with Wok-Seared Squid, 67
Short Ribs, 185-86
Shrimp: in Benne Seed Shrimp, 77; in
     Thai Seafood Salad, 102; rock, in
     Sweet Corn Fricassee, 120; with
     Serrano wrapped Mahi-Mahi,
     137; in Seafood Pot, 138; with
     sausage, 141
Shrimp and Sausage with Grape
     Tomatoes, Mint and Garlic Broth
     and Goat Cheese Grits, **140**-41;
     wine for, 248
Sirachi, in Spicy Tuna Roll, 48
Smoked Pork Stock: 34; with Scallops
     and Braised Bacon, 69; in Bacon
     Braised Greens, 165
Smoked Salmon Wellington with
     Gruyère Potato Fondue, Asparagus
     and Lemon Beurre Blanc, **126**-28;
     wine for, 247
Smoked Turkey with Bacon Braised
     Greens and Natural Jus, 164-65
Soave Classico Pra "Monte Grande",
     248
Soffrito: 27; with Braised Wreckfish,
     133; in Seafood Pot, 138
Soufflé, Grand Marnier, 228-30
Soup: Thai Coconut Chicken, 109;
     Lobster Bisque, 113; Asian
     Chicken Noodle Soup, 116; Chilled
     Tomato Soup with Crab, 117;
     Butternut Squash Soup, 119;
     Chilled Pea Soup with Lobster, 121
Sour Soy Vinaigrette: 97; in Beef
     Spring Rolls, 66
Soy: Black Bean, 22; Citrus, 22; Chili,
     22; Yuzu, 49; in Ginger-Soy Butter,
     56
Soy Caramel, 155
Soybeans, green. *See* Edamame.
Soy-Glazed Shiitake Mushrooms, 43

Spiced Peaches, 59

Spices, dry, 27

Spinach, baby: for Portobello Mille-Feulle, 101

Squash Blossom Butter: 25; with " Eggplant, Baby Squash and Tomatoes, 133

Squash Blossoms: in butter, 25; steamed, with Ginger Pork and Chanterelles, 75; tempura-fried, 133

Squash, baby, 133

Squash, butternut: in soup, 119; in risotto, 156

Squid: Wok-Seared, with Chili Soy and Shiso, 67; in Thai Seafood Salad, 102

Steak Diane with Roasted Mushrooms, Gruyère Potato Fondue and Truffle Cracked Peppercorn Cream, **180**-81; wine for, 247

Steamed Squash Blossoms with Ginger Pork and Chanterelles, **74**-75; wine for, 246

Stew, Bacon and Oyster, 116

Stocks: Veal, 31; Chicken, 32; Roasted Duck, 33; Smoked Pork, 34; Fortified (Quick), 34; Shellfish, 35; Fish Fumet, 35

Strawberry Dust, 233

Succotash Fricassee: 202; with Scallops and Braised Bacon, 69

Sweating, 242

Sweet Corn Fricassee, 129

Sweet Potatoes, Truffle, 162

Swordfish, grilled, 146-47

Syrups: Balsamic, 92; Port Wine, 101; Maple, 119; vanilla bean, 233; Mint, 237

Szechwan Pepper Crusted Tuna with Jerusalem Artichokes, Mizuna, Braised Belgian Endive, Capers and Feta, **148**-49; wine for, 248

Szechwan peppercorns, 59, 149, 185

Tartare: Tuna, 43; Beef, 49

Tempura Batter: with Avocado and Soft-Shell Crab Roll, 71; Squash Blossoms fried in, 133; with Veal Oscar and Soft-Shell Crab, 189

Testing for Doneness, 243

Thai Coconut Chicken, **108**-9; wine for, 246

Thai Coconut Cream, 139

Thai Seafood Salad, 102; wine for, 248

Thai Spice: 185; in Thai Seafood Salad, 102; in Thai Coconut Chicken, 109

Thai-Spiced Short Rib and Lobster with Edamame, Shiitake Mushrooms, Teardrop Tomatoes and Celery Root Purée, **184**-87; wine for, 247

Tilefish, Seared Golden, 139

Toast Points: Brioche, 49, 100; with baguettes, 89

Toasted Walnuts, 87

Toffee, 233

Tokaji Aszu Disnoko 5 Puttonyos, 246

Tomato Soup, Chilled, 117

Tomatoes, grape: with Bay Scallop Ceviche, 46; in Garden and Herb Salad, 95; with Braised Wreckfish, 133, with Serrano Wrapped Mahi-Mahi, 137; in Seafood Pot, 138; with Shrimp and Sausage, 141; with Palmetto Bass, 145

Tomatoes, green: in Green Tomato-Wasabi Cocktail Sauce, 47, 56

Tomatoes, heirloom: with Lobster BLT, 81

Tomatoes, plum: in Chilled Tomato Soup, 117

Tomatoes, yellow teardrop: in Garden and Herb Salad, 95; in Chilled Tomato Soup, 117; with Shrimp and Sausage, 141; with Palmetto Bass, 145; in Thai Spiced Short Ribs and Lobster, 185-86

Truffle Butter: 26; in Truffle Grit Cakes, 78, 137; in Truffle Sweet Potatoes, 162

Truffle Cracked Peppercorn Cream, 181

Truffle Essence Arugula, 57

Truffle Grits Cakes: with Butter-Poached Lobster, 78; with Serrano Wrapped Mahi-Mahi, 137

Truffle Sweet Potatoes, 162

Tuna, sashimi: with Kumomoto Oysters with Cilantro Lime Glaze and Pine-apple Wasabi, 41; Asian, Tartare, with Cucumbers, Chili Glaze,

Shiitake Mush-rooms and Chinese Flatbread, 43; in Deconstructed Spicy Tuna Roll, 48; in Crisp Wasabi Tuna, 131; Szechwan, 149

Tuna and Oysters, 246

Tuna Tartare, 246

Turkey, Smoked, 164

Udon noodles, in Asian Chicken Noodle Soup, 116

Vanilla Bean Simple Syrup, 233

Veal breast, 188

Veal Oscar with Asparagus, Crispy Soft-Shell Crab and Béarnaise, **188**-91

Veal Stock: **30**-31; in Madeira Sauce, 175; in Truffle Cracked Peppercorn Cream, 181; in Celery Root Purée, 185-86; in Veal Oscar, 188; with Braised Lamb Shanks, 199

Vietnamese Spring Rolls, 246

Vilafonte "Series M", 248

Vina Sastre Ribera del Duero, 247

Vinaigrette: Walnut, 87; Garlic Shallot, 89, 95; Sour Soy, 66, 97; Mint, 121; Blood Orange, 159

Wahoo, Grilled, 129

Walnut Chutney, with cranberry, 89

Walnut Vinaigrette, 87

Walnuts, toasted, 87

Warm Molten Chocolate Cake, 231-33, **232**

Wasabi: Pineapple, 41; Cocktail Sauce with Green Tomato, 47, 56; with Tuna, 131

Watercress, with Fromage Blanc and Dried Fig Compote, 100

Waxed beans, 91

White Chocolate Sauce, 224

White Chocolate-Graham Cracker Moons, 224

Wok-Seared Squid with Chili Soy and Shiso, 67; wine for, 248

Wreckfish, Braised, 133

Yuzu Soy, 49

Zind-Humbrecht Riesling, 248